Conte

A VETERAN TEACHER'S GUIDE
to TAKING CARE *of* YOUR
STUDENTS *and* YOURSELF

In Our Classrooms

ANNE RICHTER

GREENLEAF
BOOK GROUP PRESS

Published by Greenleaf Book Group Press
Austin, Texas
www.gbgpress.com

Distributed by Greenleaf Book Group Group

For ordering information or special discounts for bulk purchases, please contact Greenleaf Book Group at PO Box 91869, Austin, TX 78709, 512.891.6100.

Design and composition by Greenleaf Book Group
Cover design by Greenleaf Book Group

Publisher's Cataloging-in-Publication data is available.

Print ISBN: 979-8-88645-391-1

eBook ISBN: 979-8-88645-392-8

To offset the number of trees consumed in the printing of our books, Greenleaf donates a portion of the proceeds from each printing to the Arbor Day Foundation. Greenleaf Book Group has replaced over 50,000 trees since 2007.

Printed in the United States of America on acid-free paper

25 26 27 28 29 30 31 32 10 9 8 7 6 5 4 3 2 1

First Edition

To the K–12 educators who show up every day for their students.

Introduction

MARCH 11, 2020

"*We are shutting down all in-person instruction for two weeks effective immediately. Go back to your classrooms and grab what you can in five minutes and go home.*" So were the startling words of our superintendent of schools that afternoon during a March 11, 2020, emergency faculty meeting.

Our middle school staff had been abuzz that entire day as the governor of New York shut down our neighboring school district, New Rochelle. Yes, in a state with almost twenty million citizens, the first person to contract COVID-19 and start the lower Westchester County and Manhattan COVID-19 spread lived less than one mile from where I resided and worked as a teacher. In a mere eight days, that one man, Patient Zero, had spread COVID-19 to over a hundred others. It would take only a few additional hours for Governor Andrew Cuomo to announce that he was effectively shutting down not only all New Rochelle School District schools but also any school within a one-mile radius of the outbreak, which included my own, in the Tuckahoe Union Free School District.

We, the faculty, were caught off guard and dazed as our superintendent finished her emergency staff meeting remarks. As the instructional staff made our way back to our classrooms, I was thinking about what materials and supplies I would be grabbing. As the STEM (science, technology, engineering, and math) and life science teacher, I knew to grab scientific tools and supplies used for labs—beakers, test tubes, chromatography paper, chromatography solvent, ethanol, Lugol's solution, and BTB, to name a few. I also realized I would need to grab all my content folders for the topics for the remainder of the school year.

Once back in my science lab, I stopped dead in my tracks. My teaching career of thirty-plus years had been built in this physical space, and I was at a loss as to what to pack for home. A few colleagues stopped by to ask what I was taking, and I told them to stop wasting time, go to their own spaces, and "grab and go" what they would need to teach their curriculum from home.

Though many colleagues were excited that we would be

"off" for two weeks, I was concerned in ways that perhaps my colleagues were not. From the standpoint of a classroom teacher, we had no other school district to look to as a blueprint for remote instruction. Teachers would be relying on district staff for establishing protocols and training and evaluating how well instruction was being conveyed—all in real time. But as a teacher with a master's degree in public health from Columbia University Mailman School of Public Health, I was all too aware that humankind was about to face the greatest public health threat in the last hundred years. A localized virus from thousands of miles away had landed in my backyard.

I was a teacher who had to transition from classroom to online teaching. I was a single parent of two: an elementary school teacher daughter and a college senior son whom I had to keep safe. I was a woman who suffered from COPD, putting me at greater risk for pneumonia infection and death, and I was a daughter of two housebound parents in their nineties. And all I knew for sure was that I was equally terrified of the knowns and the unknowns as I turned off the classroom lights and closed and locked my classroom door while balancing ten or so bags filled to their brims.

March 11, 2020, was a turning point for our world at large as an unprecedented, once-in-a-hundred-years pandemic roiled across the globe. COVID-19 brought life to a standstill. Populations grappled with acute illness and death, economic disasters—personal and professional—were rampant, and the social fabric of society frayed practically overnight. Health-care workers, first responders, police, firefighters, transportation workers, and other "essential workers" in food production and food delivery, commerce, critical retail, and trades were celebrated as heroes. As schools shut down across our country, America's teachers, also identified as essential workers, faced our own set of challenges, fears, and successes.

Working, earning a salary, and receiving health benefits as teachers during this global health crisis was no small miracle. Yet the way we interacted with our students and delivered our instruction, learned new skill sets seemingly overnight, and coped with the effects of the pandemic on ourselves and our family members put enormous stress on us as a collective professional organization.

Five years out from living through the pandemic, teachers are still reeling from its effects. Since 2022, graduate schools have reported yearly decreases in students entering K–12 teaching degree programs, and teachers leaving the profession for reasons other than retirement have skyrocketed. School districts across America are finding it near impossible to fill current vacancies.[1]

Teachers who have stayed in their classes post-pandemic report increasingly stressful work environments as we face the unprecedented rise of old and new—yet increasingly common—school crises. In America, school shootings tragically continue to be the most catastrophic and prepared-for crisis. "In the first year of the pandemic, when schools were closed, there was a major decline in gun violence incidents on school grounds. Since then, recent years saw a stark increase in school shootings, with 2021, 2022, 2023 and 2024 all setting records since at least 2008. There were at least 83 incidents in 2024, but 2022 was one of the deadliest years, with 47 fatalities."[2]

These staggering statistics make it imperative that schools hold staff-mandated workshops and student reviews of emergency procedures specific to every classroom and physical space they inhabit throughout their school day. Staff and students also participate in mandatory drills at least four times a year. During these practice drills, teachers must maintain an air of calming control so as to not frighten or upset our students while being cognizant of the fact that a real threat can occur in any school, including our own. Drills are necessary but add to the stressors teachers experience.

Whereas school shootings were a fact of school life before the pandemic, now student anxiety issues rank as a major crisis that teachers and school staff grapple with daily. The *Youth Risk Behavior Survey Data Summary & Trends Report: 2013–2023* highlights concerning trends about the mental health of US high school students. In 2023, 40 percent had persistent feelings of sadness or hopelessness. In 2023, 20 percent of students seriously considered attempting suicide, and nearly 10 percent attempted suicide.[3]

The data revealing the level of mental health distress many students are feeling constitutes a crisis. In response, teachers are reminded to continue fostering positive connections, watch for signs of distress in students, and refer students to school support when needed—all in the hope that these strategies will protect student mental health. Though this is a critically needed role that teachers can fill, being responsible for triaging our students' mental health adds to teachers' stress levels—so much so that "78 percent of public schools reported providing increased social and emotional support for staff in response to increased stressors since the pandemic."[4] We may have survived teaching through the pandemic, but the experience has changed us and reshaped the profession we have dedicated our lives to.

Teachers: We chose this incredibly difficult and rewarding profession. Now as individual educators and a collective professional organization, we are at a post-pandemic crossroads, which brings us to the "why" of this book you have chosen to read.

Within these pages, teacher-colleagues, I have posed difficult but necessary questions for us to examine what we experienced teaching through the crisis of COVID-19, what we learned, what we can apply to any crisis moving forward, what it takes to be a classroom teacher, and our changing roles in our school communities today. You will hear from K–12 teachers across America validating our experiences. I will provide concrete strategies for meeting any crisis that may arise in our day-to-day classroom life. Key takeaways will speak to your personal and professional growth. This book is designed to focus on you, to allow you to be the very best teacher you can be so our students can be their best and so our profession and its members can be respected for the critical work we do. But most importantly, I hope this book reignites your passion and purpose as a classroom teacher.

Though the pandemic has passed, perhaps the most vital lesson we take forward with us is that teaching is an essential profession—during a crisis and every day. Those of us in front of the classrooms must be ready for whatever may come.

Part 1

CLASS IS IN SESSION

Every so often I will be standing dead center in my classroom, explaining a concept, telling a funny story, giving direction, praising student successes, or modeling a specific science skill, when I realize every pair of student eyes is locked on my face, listening intently to my words, and absorbing what I am trying to share with them. Surprisingly, this is both a frightening and exhilarating moment wrapped into one for a teacher.

I never thought about, trained for, or expected to be a middle school/high school classroom teacher, and yet here I am, in my thirty-fifth year teaching life science and STEM.

Over these incredible years, I have come to realize that the passion and purpose teachers bring transform students' lives and that teachers grow and learn just as much as their students. And as we tout our students' accomplishments, we need to tout our own.

Come on in, class is in session.

LESSON 1

Find Your Calling

The college awards ceremony invitation brought me back ten years. A student I had taught in seventh-grade English language arts was receiving a writing award along with her bachelor of arts degree in English from a local college. Though I had not seen or spoken to this young woman in almost ten years, she was part of the very first group of students I had stood before as a new classroom teacher in 1989. This young woman had arrived that October from the Caribbean after the devastation of Hurricane Hugo had destroyed her home island. She was part of a small group of similar students who arrived to live with relatives, and though their math skills were strong, their reading levels were at least two grade levels below seventh grade. It was my job to motivate these transplanted children and teach them to read as close to their seventh-grade level as possible by April for the New York State English Language Arts exam. This group was highly motivated and rose to my challenge, and within five months, they had each reached their reading-on-grade-level goals. Over the years, I lost touch with this special group, until Alvita's invitation gave me the opportunity to reconnect.

Alvita, in addition to winning the senior writing award, was given the honor of sharing her personal narrative at the graduation ceremony. She wrote about being a frightened thirteen-year-old in a new country, unable to read proficiently or even put sentences together with much meaning. She wrote of a teacher who had never taught children before yet channeled energy, motivation, and hope into her students by showing up every day to open their world to written language. Alvita spoke of her teacher's passion for her students and equally for the importance of reading and writing. Alvita shared that, even after all these years, she still remembered her teacher's purpose in showing up every day—to make a tangible difference in her students' lives, to make sure each one of them was able to read and write effectively and on grade level, which in turn would provide them their best chance of future success. Alvita told the audience that she would be starting her master's degree in writing in the fall, a dream that could not be realized without that teacher. Alvita concluded with her hope that every student have at least one Mrs. Richter in their lifetime, because a teacher's passion and purpose will change a student's life like nothing else can.

Reflecting on her words now, I vividly remember those children showing up at my classroom door three times a day for a total of three hours of reading instruction. As Alvita remarked, each student saw their teacher's relentless drive, but did any of those children fully understand *the crisis* behind their teacher's motivation, that seventh graders were only able to read on a fourth- or fifth-grade level? Probably not.

As students grapple with academic crises, their teachers respond with passion and purpose. Teachers are experts in managing these types of crises and can quickly map out the best and most specific instructional strategies and assignments for individual students. Our creativity is at peak to keep these students engaged and motivated to do the hard work. Our purpose is to always provide the tools and pathways for student success. When teachers are tested by different or larger-scale crises, like COVID-19, our immediate response is to dig even deeper for solutions, resolute in our purpose, and our enthusiasm is contagious.

Are You in a Profession That Speaks to You?

I have been an educator for grades 7–12 since 1989. I am qualified to teach biology, general sciences, English, health, and STEM, and I have a supervision and administration degree for both school and district leadership. In addition to my teaching responsibilities, I have written curricula for district science and other courses, mentored new teachers, advised district clubs, and served as a union representative. I spent the first ten years of my teaching career in the Northeast Bronx, New York, instructing seventh through eighth graders in English and life science in one of the most challenging middle schools in all of New York City. In 1990, I was named Rookie Teacher of the Year for my school district. For the past twenty-two years, I have instructed middle and high school life science, biology, and STEM students in a suburban school district just north of New York City.

Looking back at my thirty-five-year teaching career (which is still going strong), I cannot imagine a more creative, energizing, and gratifying way to spend my professional days. Yet teaching was never my intended profession. I didn't realize I had the intrinsic passion and purpose for it, and I didn't even consider this as my life's work until after I was already established in another professional career.

As a young child, I wanted my profession to be in health care. I graduated from Barnard College and entered the Columbia University Mailman School of Public Health, where I graduated with honors with a master's degree in public health, with concentrations in maternal and child health and hospital administration. I had many unique positions before landing at a long-term care facility in the Northeast Bronx, serving as the youngest director of a large and diverse department. Part of my hospital responsibilities was running the school-to-work program where at-risk Bronx students were given paying jobs at our facility if they attended school regularly. Each afternoon, as local children walked through our hospital doors to work with our elderly population, I recognized that these two populations needed the most attention. These students needed guidance, support, mentorship, and direction. The elderly needed comprehensive medical care, companionship, and validation that they were still valuable members of society. Around this same time, I began to realize how difficult it would be to raise a family and climb to a top hospital administrative position.

In the summer of 1989, during a serious teacher shortage, the New York City Board of Education was recruiting new teachers, with the only criteria being that a recruit had to be "a college graduate with specific numbers of credits in specific content areas." The city was allowing new recruits to enter classrooms with no education college credits, no certificates, no student teaching experience—just college credits, fingerprint checks, and the assurance that we would complete a set course of study within several years to earn official state teaching certificates.

At Barnard, I was both an English and a premedical studies major, so I had the possibility of easily earning 7–12 English and 7–12 biology teaching certificates. As it turned out, the neighborhood middle school, where many of our school-to-work students attended school, was looking for an English teacher. My true passion is in the sciences, but I took the English teaching position to, well, get my foot in the door. When I told my hospital president I was resigning to enter the teaching profession, he offered me a leave of absence, with psychiatrist sessions. I turned down his well-meaning offer and stayed for the required administrative six weeks' notice while the neighborhood school held my position open.

I finally entered that third-floor classroom at MS 113, on Barnes Avenue, in late October/early November, and I will admit that for the first month—OK, maybe two . . . OK, three months—I cried every night, sobbed as I graded papers, sobbed as I created lesson plans, which were checked by my assistant principal weekly, sobbed as I envisioned walking into the classroom as a green—lime-green—teacher. The kids knew I was a green teacher, especially my students whose time sheets I had been signing off on just a few months prior at the hospital in my cushy office with my own secretary, mind you!

But when I wasn't sobbing, I was loving every single second of my new professional life. I enjoyed being surrounded by youth, their enthusiasm was contagious, and once they realized I was on their side, they stuck to me like glue. In the city school system, competent and talented teachers are rewarded with the most academically and behaviorally challenging students. It did not matter that I had zero teaching experience; I was plopped into a classroom with seventh graders who read on a fourth-grade level, and together, we thrived. I taught English and reading during the day to those wonderful Bronx teenagers and went back to Columbia University Teachers College at night to take the first round of required education courses needed for my provisional teaching certificates. By that spring, all my seventh graders had passed their NYS Reading Exams with seventh–eighth-grade reading levels, and I was named one of two District 11 Rookie Teachers of the Year.

My first five years in the profession were hard but transformative. I still count the veteran teachers and administrators who took me under their wings as the most talented professionals I have ever encountered in a thirty-five-year career. These colleagues taught me everything there was to know about being a compassionate, fair, rigorous educator.

Within two years, I had amassed enough credits for a master's in secondary education science and was awarded tenure in my school district. A few years later, I attended graduate school at night, during the summer, and on the weekends to earn my master's in education supervision and administration. After turning down a principalship in 2003, I became a faculty member of a lower Westchester school district, and it is difficult to believe that I started my twenty-second year teaching in this particular school the fall of 2024. In total, I have been in education for thirty-five years, with a short break to be a stay-at-home mom, but even then working as a substitute teacher at a local nursery school, conducting professional development workshops at Bronx middle schools, and developing course curricula for Westchester districts.

The sobbing I first experienced seems a lifetime ago, though I lived through those new teacher experiences again when my daughter was teaching her first few years as an elementary teacher some twenty-five years after the start of my own career.

The Tears and Triumphs of Teaching

The sobs of a new teacher—or even those from an experienced educator—come from the enormous responsibility of teaching. Educators step into a classroom and must be prepared to successfully engage between 20 and 150 children each day. They must assess content mastery for every content-learning objective for every student and differentiate the same instruction for each student's individual academic and behavioral needs. Educators must ensure their learning environments are inclusive, flexible, compassionate spaces where every voice is not only heard but also listened to. They must see to it that "their kids" feel valued as students and as individuals, safe in body and psyche.

Educators must be "on" for eight hours—standing, talking, moving, encouraging, motivating, cheerleading, evaluating, troubleshooting, seeing everything, hearing everything, and all the while entertaining our diverse audience of learners. Some educators bristle at the idea that our students need to be "entertained," but as educators, we need to be able to connect with our students. Otherwise, our students will not connect with us or the content we are trying to teach.

As if all this isn't enough to make teachers sob, we also must successfully work with our students; their parents and guardians; our teaching colleagues, including co-teachers, teacher aides, department colleagues, and grade-level colleagues; custodial staff; security staff; secretarial staff; school support staff; building administrators; school board members; and district administrators.

We educators often start our days between 5:00 and 5:30 a.m. to be at school and greeting our students between 7:15 and 8:15 a.m. We are on our feet and our brains are multitasking for the next eight hours until that dismissal bell rings between 2:30 and 3:15 p.m. More often than not, our lunches go uneaten, hot coffees turn cold, and iced coffees turn lukewarm. After the dismissal bell, we attend meetings, hold student office hours, grade papers, and prepare lessons for the following day, often until 4:00 p.m. or later. Still, our workday is not done, as most educators spend an additional two to four hours in the evening prepping for the next day. These are not complaints but rather simply our realities, and we embrace them willingly.

During research for this book, I surveyed one hundred educational professionals from across the US. These educators included K–12 regular and special education classroom teachers, college professors, adult ed. instructors, ELL (English-language-learning) teachers, and teachers of adjudicated youth. These professionals were asked "How did you know being a teacher was the right fit for you?" and "What drives teachers to do the work we do?" Not surprisingly, all one hundred respondents cited their love of working with students, regardless of the student age groupings. Some responded:

"I literally walked into a first-grade classroom and got goose bumps. I never wanted to leave. I fell in love."

"If you are not in it for the children, you are in the wrong profession."

Over 80 percent of the teachers surveyed agreed that teachers nurture and prepare our students for their futures. Educators wrote "making positive differences in the lives of America's youth," "helping to guide our youth to their fullest potential," and "preparing today's youth to lead our nation into the future" as their primary reasons for going into the teaching profession and doing the work we do.

Teachers also cited one of our primary purposes in every K–12 classroom—to nurture and develop critical thinkers. "I love middle school learners. They are becoming thinkers."

So many educators had vivid recollections of individual students, like this respondent: "I spent twenty-three years working with special ed. students and regular ed. students. I still remember the first child I helped. After working with me for only a week, her mother told me that she came home and told her, 'Mama, I am not stupid. I can learn.' It literally made tears run down my face, and I never felt so proud."

Over 50 percent of those surveyed indicated that, for them, teaching was a calling, a passion that gave them purpose every day and that "a career in teaching was just meant to be."

Teaching is not for everyone, and certainly not for those looking for an easier, less time-consuming job. Teaching is not a "clock in at nine and clock out at five" type of job. Teaching is not a "leave the building, leave the work behind" type of job. In fact, teaching is not even a "job"; it is a "profession," as it requires a specific course of advanced study, training, and certifications. If you ask most educators, they will tell you that teaching is difficult and that it will take up most of your life from August through June. The exceptional educators, however, will tell you that teaching is a passion that is centered in our core—we live it and breathe it, and it consumes us much like a calling does. Though I never expected to have a thirty-five-year professional existence in a classroom, I remain flabbergasted that for me teaching *was and remains* this all-consuming, joyous, incredible, exciting passion. This is what separates the bad from the good from the truly gifted educators—those who are passionate about what they do each day, those who will say that teaching is their calling. This became all the clearer while teaching through the COVID-19 pandemic.

When Your Passion Is Tested by a Crisis

The rapidly spreading and deadly viral pandemic shut down my district in March 2020, and in less than a week, teachers were instructing remotely, both asynchronized and synchronized. Stressors were never greater. Teachers, considered essential workers, felt an obligation to keep some sense of normalcy for our students even through computer screens. We showed up, took attendance, presented truncated lessons, assigned short homework assignments, all to keep our students occupied with something other than the reality of their world becoming isolated and deadly overnight. Teachers did our best through those months of mid-March through June; though honestly, those three and a half months felt like twelve. We mourned with our students the canceled proms, award ceremonies, and graduations—not just as their teachers but also as parents to our own children whose lives were equally upended.

Returning to our school buildings in September 2020 was even more surreal. Everyone was masked up, and to this day, there are students I can still only recognize by their eyes. Students were on hybrid schedules, with half our student body in the school building sitting in front of us behind plexiglass partitions, as we teachers were as well, while the other half of the class was at home on their Zoom meetings with cameras pointed anywhere other than at their actual faces.

March 2020 through June 2021 was simply a nightmare. Students were grappling with emotional and mental health issues that left little room for academic focus, let alone progress. Academic rigor was put aside, which translated into student behavior issues spiraling out of control. Parents were overwhelmed with everything that piggybacks on a pandemic—economic uncertainty, health uncertainty, loss of any sense of control when it came to their lives and their children's lives. Parents looked to educators to help get their families through this harrowing time. Educators did the very best we could, because that is what we do and who we are—we take care of our students and partner with our parents.

Throughout the pandemic, it became clear very quickly which teachers would make it and which ones would leave the profession at the end of June. Teachers who were passionate about making a positive impact on students despite the hundred-year pandemic returned to their classrooms in September 2021 stronger, more compassionate, and better equipped to handle any other crisis that lay in our future. Teaching through COVID-19 had the effect of shaping many teachers into more resilient, effective, and reflective practitioners. These teachers did not merely survive teaching through the pandemic. They thrived as professionals because, for them, teaching was not simply a job; it was their life's passion and purpose. For other educators, the pandemic forced questions to the surface of whether teaching was the correct professional fit moving forward. For thousands of teachers across America, their answer was a resounding no, as some retired and many just quit.

Crises Bring Clarity

Crises, like COVID-19, provide opportunities for reflection and evaluation that can lead to significant changes in one's personal and professional lives. Crises are often the unexpected catalysts that give us permission to look carefully at our unique situations and decide whether this is who we still are and whether this is where we still want to be. The worst crises often provide the best opportunities to understand what is most important to us in the moment and for moving forward. For these reasons, crises bring clarity that can either reinforce what we know to be true or help us make positive changes.

KEY TAKEAWAYS

Don't wait for a crisis to find out if teaching is your calling.

- Knowing if K–12 teaching, or any professional position, is the right fit for you ultimately depends on your passion for your day-to-day professional responsibilities.
- To figure this out, take time to seriously answer these questions:
  - » Are you energized and fully engaged throughout your workday?
  - » Are you excited to be in the classroom, working alongside young people?
  - » Does your work give you purpose?
  - » Are you driven to do the work you do, even on hard days?
  - » Are you always thinking of ways to improve your work?
  - » Do you see your own value in guiding students to be their best?
  - » Moving past a crisis, are your responses to these questions the same?
- An intrinsic desire, or passion, to do your life's work is the key to personal growth, inner success, and professional gratification.

- Crises—both grand and small scale—can prompt you to question your life choices.
- Embrace moments of self-reflection that often lead to clarity.
- Look past your present to your future and don't settle for anything less.

LESSON 2

Performing Five Shows a Day

Teachers are performers, only with a much tougher audience than, let's say, those seeing *Hamilton* on Broadway. Our student audience members don't necessarily want to be physically in the class. Our students don't necessarily like the content, have any interest in the content, or even understand the content. Students may not even like the teacher standing in front of them in the class, for that matter. Teachers must welcome our students; assess if there are any issues that need to be handled before class; make every student feel valued, safe—physically and emotionally—and academically vested in the content and their academic success; and make them want to come back tomorrow. In elementary school, that may be 25 students for 6 *long* hours a day. In middle/high school, that is approximately 30 students per period for 5 periods per day. That is a total of 150 students each day, every day.

Teaching style is born from and an extension of your personality, and all teachers have styles that best suit them. Regardless of a teacher's unique style, however, all teachers must be able to connect with students on a personal level, bring an energy level that engages students in the content and instruction, and make style adjustments in response to what might be happening in that learning moment.

As I mentor teachers entering the field, a common question I hear from them is how to shape your own teaching style to meet student personalities, learning needs, and any pop-up crises. My response is often "take your lead from your students or the crisis at hand." My teaching style has always been high-octane-energy level, starting at 7:30 a.m., literally dancing in the hallway with other teachers as I greet still-groggy students. Although an energetic greeting works to engage many of my students, this style does not mesh with many of my on-the-spectrum students who prefer low voices and dimmed lighting within soothing classroom spaces. Therefore, to meet all student needs, I will adjust my tone, range, and projection of voice; skip the dancing; and turn off some classroom lights once

I see a student drawing into themselves in response to my high energy. Knowing my style is not always for all, I often distribute teacher/classroom style questionnaires to all incoming students so I can better understand how my teaching style can best complement their learning styles and personalities.

The most important aspects of any teaching style are consistency, effective management, and leadership. Students must expect the same classroom routines, expectations, and consequences every day class is in session. Students must intrinsically know the teacher is in charge. The teacher must be capable of positively interacting with all students with respect, affection, and authority and able to handle any type of crisis with professionalism and leadership. Whether the crisis is an unexpected school evacuation due to a boiler problem or an unexpected hold in place to allow the custodians to capture and relocate a squirrel who found itself inside the school, all students look to their classroom teacher for instruction, calm, collectedness, and comfort.

Planning Prepares Teachers for Every Lesson

In the beginning days of my teaching career, each week, teachers had to submit their lesson plans to our assistant principal. Though it was time consuming, I knew then that these lessons would become the basis of my curriculum moving forward. This bothersome task was a blessing in disguise for those who took it seriously, though many did not.

Lesson plans are the foundation for what you will be achieving each instructional period. Lesson plans are a reflection of your teaching, instructional, and organizational style. Lesson plans should include academic objectives, key content and skills, instructional activities, evaluation tools, lesson extensions, and grading rubrics.

As a new teacher, I saw all content areas—including English, social studies, science, math, art, music, technology, and languages—as fluid, and I knew lessons had to reflect this every day. A veteran social studies teacher I worked with all those years ago kept a binder full of handwritten lessons in faded pencil that he used every year for over twenty-five years. However, those history lessons did not reflect any world changes that had happened in real time. This teacher's students knew they were not getting the most out of their class and took their concerns to other teachers, as well as school administration. Little changed that year, but the teacher did retire soon after. As a new educator, I knew enough to absorb what worked for successful teachers and incorporate those practices into my own professional toolbox as well as to avoid strategies that I saw to be ineffective.

Throughout my career, I learned that lessons had to be engaging for both students and the teacher—me. The only way to incorporate content fluidity without losing your own interest and your students' interest is through creativity and engagement, much like live performers hold their audience members' attention. Teachers often use only one method of delivering instruction when their approach should be varied. Classroom learning communities shouldn't be solely teacher centered or authoritative, with the teacher being center stage, the "true expert" in delivering content, while students are passive participants, simply listening. Though teacher lectures for content and skill introduction are necessary, teachers should be sure to serve as facilitators during subsequent student-learning engagement through inquiry-based, student-driven group-learning activities.

Once you have your architectural blueprint for a lesson, it is very easy to adapt, and in many cases totally rework, lessons, which is what was needed during the COVID-19 crisis. Overnight, teachers were expected to instruct students using only computer-based activities. Established lesson plans allowed teachers to quickly and easily adapt existing activities into online assignments. Students lost no instructional downtime due to their teachers being able to seamlessly convert traditional in-person lessons into live, digital lessons.

The Teacher Balancing Act: The "How" Is Just as Important as the "What"

How do teachers successfully engage students? There are so many different components to "teaching style" that I generally advise developing teachers to watch, learn, and absorb what works for successful veteran educators. The most successful teachers are always the fun and energetic ones. Students know the "funny ones," the "ones who tell the best stories," and the "ones who make learning fun."

Each morning when students arrive on the third floor of my school, they see many of their teachers dancing and calling out "good morning"s to students by name. Students are invited to join us; some do, others smile and watch, and a few roll their eyes. But if we teachers are ever late to "dancing in the square," students come looking for us to start their morning. All successful teachers find ways to connect with their students by talking sports, music, or even current events. In classrooms, visitors will see teachers as facilitators with high student engagement through a multitude of instructional practices. Time flies when you are having fun, and class periods often pass so quickly that students are heard saying, "Wait, we just got here!"

In addition, veteran educators agree that without strong classroom management with clear academic and behavioral expectations, no learning or student progress can be made. It must be noted that teachers with classroom-management expertise can still be the funny, energetic, and fun teachers. Surveyed teachers shared the following about the importance of classroom management:

- "Set the class tone and rules immediately."

- "*Respect* and *listening* should be the two words students live by."
- "Strictness is not meanness; it is having the students know their behavioral expectations."
- "Consistent structure with much compassion and love."

As crucial as classroom management is to instructional delivery, teachers must be mindful that what impacts our students, as individuals and collectively, impacts our class routines, structure, and lesson goals. We must be flexible to adjust our teaching styles to student-centered issues. Even this veteran teacher knows keeping students focused on learning the days before Christmas vacation is near impossible, which is why I assign the "fun and tasty" animal cell model lab using candy on these days. Students are demonstrating a higher level of cell structure knowledge by building a model while in a slightly more relaxed environment, and then they are allowed to eat their candy cell after I have checked their work.

Educators: Never lose sight that teaching is an interactive collaboration between yourselves and your students. Confident and experienced teachers should always go back to their student audience for honest and direct lesson evaluations.

Last year, I developed a new instructional group project focused on the types of unicellular organisms, protists, found in freshwater environments. Student groups were provided with specific task questions, online resources, rubrics, and exemplar samples of finished products. Though students worked collaboratively to complete their group assignments, the relatively quiet and subdued students gave me pause to think they were not enjoying this new project. I had the students stop their assignments and provide me with feedback on the design and project scope. Students did not hold back their critiques of the "boring topic" and "not-challenging-enough tasks." After thanking them, I offered a choice: Finish the project as designed or work within your group to address the "not-challenging-enough tasks." Every student group reworked the assignments to make them more interesting and rigorous. This year, the student-modified project will be assigned.

Teachers have the best intentions when designing instructional activities, and yet sometimes we fall short of the bar we set. A lesson that has worked for years may no longer work for a specific group of learners. A major crisis like COVID-19 forced teachers to evaluate their instructional activities in a different light. Teachers, if you are not sure whether your instruction is engaging, ask your audience what is working for them and what is not, then make the necessary changes to ensure your students are vested in their learning every teaching moment. Invite a colleague to informally observe the lesson for feedback. I have even sought out administrators for feedback on instructional activities.

Teacher survey respondents also note "equally important to teaching style is to understand the learning styles of each of our students. Some are visual, auditory, reading/writing, and kinesthetic." Maureen P. notes that our "teaching styles must be aligned with how our students learn best. Teachers are in the classroom for our students' success, after all." When I lesson plan, I include instructional activities geared to each type of learning style so all students can feel successful. For every lesson I develop, there is a short introductory video clip, slides with both images and bulleted notes, reading assignments with corresponding comprehension questions, and a hands-on creative lab or project component.

Teaching style is most significantly influenced by the genuine connections between teachers, students, student families, and the larger school community. In order to successfully engage students in the classroom, we have to make the effort to engage with them in "outside the classroom" school activities. Nothing strengthens a teacher–student bond more than showing up at their volleyball game or debate tournament or chaperoning the school's Winter Ball. When I was that first-year teacher in the Bronx, I was invited to my students' homes for dinners and even Sweet Sixteen celebrations—and yes, after confirming parents would be present, I attended! Teachers: Step out of your classrooms to see your students as the incredibly talented and multifaceted young people they all are. Seeing your student as a "whole child" provides you with deeper insights as to how they interact and learn. Students will see that you are invested in them as individuals and as young people, and they will want to make you proud—both in and out of the classroom. Your teaching style will be enriched by these special connections.

Virtual Performances and Mask-erades

When the pandemic caused schools to shut down, remote teaching and learning became the new way. It was difficult at best and impossible at worst. Computer screens were a physical barrier that teachers never had experience with. Students would often not turn on their video, we could not see their faces in their darkened bedrooms, or cameras were pointed toward the ceiling. Many teachers came to know which student had logged into the class just by the sound of their barking dog, the TV show playing in the background, or their customized Zoom background. It took a few weeks just for teachers to figure out the technology behind remote learning, and a class session did not go by without one tech mishap or another.

On top of the difficulties created by this sudden transition to remotely delivered lessons, we also had to continue to teach content and engage students while they struggled with the stress and anxiety of the pandemic. My "five shows a day" included tours of my house and computer cameos of my dog Sadie. I showed my students a sign I had made for my front door:

DO NOT DISTURB
No Ringing Bell or Knocking
Educating America's Youth

From mid-March to the end of June, we showed up on screen each day, but creating engaging lessons was a challenge.

Once we got back into the classroom in the fall of 2020, teachers and students were masked, sitting behind plexiglass shields, and placed six feet apart. This made it impossible to connect like I was used to doing with my students. I would like to tell you that teachers, including myself, were able to quickly and easily find new ways to engage students in their learning, but for many educators, this was still incredibly difficult, though we all still tried.

Connections with our students were still challenging to make, and there was little silliness and fun. Teaching was *hard* in ways never experienced, and trying to get to know students, engage them, and have them interested in content—let alone master it—was brutal for colleagues, myself, and our students. Most times, teachers were satisfied with simply being in the classroom, reassuring students that sooner rather than later school would get back to normal, because a lot of students couldn't see ever getting back to "normal." They had lunch at desks set up in the gymnasium, outdoor recess only when the weather permitted, staggered dismissals, and smaller classes, with half the students in school and the other half out, and often best friends were in the *other* cohort.

I felt and knew that I was no longer the teacher I used to be. No morning dance greetings allowed, fewer funny stories to tell, little silliness, and no group work, as I was up at the front of the classroom sitting behind a computer simply spewing content at my scared and bored and lonely students. Dare I admit that teachers, including myself, were also feeling bored, lonely, and even a bit scared too? We were experiencing our professional lives turned upside down and wondered when it was all going to end. Is it any wonder that so many educators questioned their professional choices during this year?

Yet, throughout those trying teaching moments, I tried to let my uniqueness shine and bring a bit of lightness to a dark period. My students got a kick out of the fact that every day I color-coordinated a mask to each of my outfits. There were many days I chose a single color and dressed in it from head to toe. Dance parties were out of the question, but every Wednesday, class began with karaoke up on the class SMART Board, and we sang loudly, and often off-key. Friday lessons began with "Funny Friday," where students could tell jokes or pose riddles.

Students were encouraged to create two-minute "Teach Your Pet Some Science" videos, which were played in class for small prizes. One student put their mom's work lab coat on Winnie, the family Weimaraner dog, who "explained" the structures of a human bone. The class was pretty sure the explanation came from the student herself, who was off camera, but class consensus was that Winnie needed her own YouTube channel. Students were also tasked with creating plant cell models using only materials found inside their homes or in their yards, taking a picture, and sharing. One student used only natural materials from her yard, including leaves, vines, rocks, flowers, and stems, to create a true work of art. During the holiday season, I asked students to get out of their bedrooms and set themselves in front of some holiday decorations, which added great screen cheer and showcased many beautifully decorated Christmas trees, creatively themed Hanukkah menorahs, and hand-carved Kwanzaa kinara.

Five years later, I see these same students, now high school juniors and seniors, in school hallways, and they still thank me for getting them through an impossible year. These young people tell me I *was* silly, I *did tell* the funniest stories, and I *did make* learning fun. My advice then is even when you do not seem to be making an impact, allow your unique teaching style to lead the way.

Shaping your own teaching style is a fluid, ever-changing evolution that takes years. No matter the situation, simply show up in your classroom to do the best job you can at that moment.

KEY TAKEAWAYS

Always show up with your best, most authentic self to make the most meaningful student connections.

- Watch, learn, and absorb what works for successful educators.
- Catalog every lesson, activity, project, and assessment you create for the length of your teaching career for lesson continuity and ease of adaptability when needed.
- Teaching is an interactive collaboration between teacher and students.
- Teachers use humor and common interests to make learning fun and accessible to all learners and to connect with students.
- Teaching style must include consistency, effective classroom management, and leadership, especially during and after a crisis, so students know they are being taken care of by a calm, able professional.

LESSON 3

Embracing Professional Growth

Since 2009, my school district has been a cutting-edge leader in the use of technology, both in teaching tools and student learning devices. For the past fifteen years, every classroom has been outfitted with the latest SMART Boards/BenQ Boards, wireless keyboards, HoverCams, the newest desktops with attendance and gradebook programs, numerous apps, and touch screen Chromebooks. I wish I could say that I and my students have benefited from my district's investment in these incredible tools from their introduction. Always uncomfortable with technology, I was reluctant to embrace these devices and a new skill set until I was forced to under great stress in a moment of unprecedented crisis.

Teachers must know what skill sets, instructional practices, and expertise we bring into our classrooms since these comprise the work we do. And periodically we must evaluate them to see what we need to keep, tweak, throw out, or even learn. This professional self-reflection was certainly necessary during COVID-19, but this practice should be done regularly, not simply in crises, so we can be the very best classroom teachers for our students so they can achieve and succeed each day.

Identify Your Strengths and Weaknesses

The first step in evaluating professional skills and practices is to identify your strengths and weaknesses. This is a necessary first step, as it brings into focus specific skills or practices that are still working or require tweaking and that you do not even have and need to acquire. Many articles and books have been written on this topic alone. Generally, you need to review your educational and work expertise, complete specific assessments, solicit constructive feedback from trusted and respected colleagues, articulate and set reasonable goals, and track your progress. But nothing tests and reveals teacher strengths and weaknesses more than a crisis.

MY NEMESIS—TECHNOLOGY

When I started teaching in my current school in 2003, my classroom, like all classrooms, had chalkboards, overhead projectors, TVs on movable stands, and a large desktop computer that was used basically as a word processor. By 2009, these outdated, time-consuming, slow instructional and recordkeeping tools were being replaced with state-of-the-art, faster, more efficient technologies.

I always felt intimidated by technology. To mask my underlying fear, I would claim to colleagues and administrators alike that my reluctance came from "my brain not being wired for technology." I must have been convincing because I was literally the *last* teacher in my building to receive their first SMART Board, and my principal at that time sent me to a special summer training program on how to use it! Even with the specialized training, it took me years to use that original SMART Board with ease. Using technology to deliver instruction was easier and faster, saved time, and engaged students who had been raised on screens, yet I was still resistant.

When my district announced in 2014 that we were becoming a one-to-one district—a Chromebook for every student in grades 6–12—I was not supportive of the initiative and voiced my concerns. I argued that research showed that students recalled information better by writing notes rather than reading teacher-posted online notes. I offered research showing student social behavior changes due to excessive screen time, and now our students would be staring at screens during school hours too. District leadership listened to my concerns and those of other teachers, yet every student was issued a Chromebook nevertheless. In hindsight, I wonder if I had embraced technology, used it, and collected my own student data on the positives and negatives of its daily use in our classrooms, would my concerns have been heard and perhaps given more weight? It is not lost on me that now, in 2025, districts across the country, including my own, are taking tangible steps to limit student screen time in a push for more social interactions among our students. Still, in 2014, when I was still uncomfortable using technology, my school tech coaches were extremely patient with me as I peppered them with tons of questions on Chromebook, Google Classroom, posting assignments, grading assignments, and the like.

From 2015 to 2019, I slowly integrated Google Classroom into my day-to-day instruction, increasingly assigned online assignments through Google Docs, created digital seating charts, used online gradebooks, and posted regularly on my district web page. I was not any more comfortable or even skilled with the technology I was using, but I used it grudgingly, because these were district technology mandates. Technology was still my nemesis, my one major professional weakness, as evidenced by my reluctance to use it, my reluctance to become proficient in the use of it, and the many, many times tech coaches had to correct my online errors.

However, technology was here to stay, and my hesitation to embrace technology as both a teaching and learning tool could only last so long—even I knew this. What I did not know was that a once-in-a-lifetime pandemic would be the catalyst for my professional growth, changing an instructional weakness into an instructional strength.

COVID-19—AN OPPORTUNITY FOR PROFESSIONAL GROWTH

When the COVID-19 lockdown became a reality on Wednesday, March 11, 2020, it took our superintendent only one day to send out a district-wide email stating we were transitioning to "synchronous remote instruction" the following Monday. This meant that all teachers would be teaching "live" through Zoom or Google Meet links on Monday, March 16. With little more than a weekend to prepare, I realized that if I was to connect with my students and try to provide the best educational experience, which is "my why" for teaching, under these dire circumstances, then technology was the *only* way I was going to accomplish this. At that moment, sitting in my living room surrounded by unpacked reusable bags filled with my classroom supplies, I knew I could no longer fear using technology. I could no longer push it away. Instead, I made a conscious decision to reframe my thinking about technology. I was now determined to embrace technology.

I was determined to learn everything there was to know about technology and how to use it to my and my students' best advantage. Technology was now going to be my inspiration, the catalyst for creating new instructional activities to engage my students during this period of online learning. Now all I needed was to find resources and strategies to become a tech expert.

Identifying Resources and Strategies to Help Your Professional Growth

As teachers, we have access to a multitude of high-quality resources no matter the area of professional growth you are interested in. Many school districts have teacher mentors, curriculum chairs, peer coaches, and tech coaches specifically for the professional growth of staff. When you are trying to identify the best resources for your needs, these are the people and organizations you should turn to first. There are also many professional journals, professional organizations, local teacher centers that offer professional development courses, and school district professional development courses.

My own district had a wealth of resources on "tech proficiency and uses in the classroom," and the weekend before remote instruction began for the COVID-19 shutdown, I read through as many articles and watched as many district training videos as I could squeeze in. I watched and rewatched each posted "how to" video. Over the next weeks and remaining months in our school year, I spent hours reviewing my paper science labs and tweaking them to online formats. I did the same for student assignments. I used my HoverCam to record lesson videos so I could post these for student review and reference. I scoured every print and digital newspaper for how best to dress for Zoom and for the best lighting, best headsets, and best microphones to use for online presentations and live feeds. Amazon boxes were arriving daily—ring lights, laptop stands, headsets, black turtlenecks. My son, a college senior also forced home, became my personal on-site tech trainer and troubleshooter. He set up and showed me how to have a minimum of two screens running at one time.

I became an expert at Google Meets and Zoom meetings, running two screens at once, sharing screens, freezing screens, even interjecting HoverCam shots. I used Screencastify, a district video-making app, to make videos of every lesson I taught online. I made weekly videos of "Just Checking In," often with my dog Sadie, and posted them for students to watch and leave comments. My school tech coaches would check in regularly to ask if I had any questions, to which I replied, "No, I am good," when, in fact, I was great! Once I made the decision to embrace my fear of technology, it became my source of professional and personal growth.

Professional Growth Realized

When we returned to in-person instruction the following September, technology was still the most important tool to drive instruction and learning. Our students were in split shifts, and although we finally had actual students sitting in the classrooms with us again, our focus was still on those students who were on screen, because we needed to make sure they were present and engaged in all learning activities. Teachers were expected to be tech proficient and savvy and use all the available tech tools to continue to reach our digital audiences.

One concrete indicator of my professional growth came in the winter of 2021. Imagine my surprise and sense of accomplishment when I was notified by Screencastify that I was the top producer of lesson videos for my entire school district, recording over one hundred lesson videos. In these student-driven learning moments, I realized I had certainly grown professionally in technology usage, to the benefit of my students. Not only was I proficient in the use of technology, but I was also confident in my own tech abilities.

Recently, my district was switching out older SMART Boards for new BenQ Boards. This time around, I specifically asked the director of technology if I could be moved to the top of the replacement list. When my board was switched out, I came in early each day and stayed late after school to run "how to" videos on my Chromebook while navigating the BenQ Board, essentially teaching myself how to use this new technology. My initiative was also noticed by my students, who voiced how proud they were of me for my efforts and gains in proficiency. Of course, there are still those moments when my students troubleshoot tech issues for me, which builds their confidence while teaching me a new skill.

Technology, an instructional and learning tool, may have become essential to the practice of teaching due to the COVID-19 crisis, but this tool remains the primary way teachers instruct and students learn today. A professional goal that I set for myself almost five years ago was realized in part by the professional development I purposefully sought out, consistently used, and still add to today. Goals realized will help you navigate through a crisis, but goals realized also help you succeed every day in the classroom.

Professional Goals Can Lead to Creative Outlets

Embracing my professional goal of becoming technology proficient also opened the next chapter in my professional and personal life—writing a book, starting a consulting business, and creating an online educational resource website.

My experiences teaching and the lessons I learned through the crisis of COVID-19, including my professional development journey, prompted me to start journaling nightly—yes, pen to paper, in long hand—which led to me writing a manuscript, which ultimately became this book you are reading. Among the many things I learned in my journey to technological mastery is that using the latest tech tools does not mean you no longer use low-tech tools. My practice of taking pen to paper has always been my go-to method, and it will remain so. Having more tools in your toolbox affords you the choice of what tool to use when.

Becoming comfortable with technology also allowed me to literally design my own educational website, www.InOurClassrooms.com. Technology has allowed me to create an educational consulting business and connect with clients both near and far. These creative endeavors would never have been realized without that initial professional growth goal of embracing technology.

Level Up Your Teaching

No one was more amazed than I was at just how totally driven to learn technology I became during the pandemic, but be sure, my learning is far from over. During class recently, I was having difficulty toggling between different types of documents. Students were trying to walk me through the steps, but I was not having much success. They came to the consensus that I was "unteachable."

I was shocked and a bit hurt that they gave up on me so quickly. I calmly asked the class whether they could ever imagine me, or any teacher, telling them that they were "unteachable." Could they ever imagine me, or any teacher, giving up so quickly when teaching them a new skill or concept? I explained to my students that yes, it takes me longer to learn tech skills than it may take other people, especially young people, that I simply don't understand how to do this computer task "yet," but that I would get it with guidance and practice as long as they didn't give up on me. They didn't, and I did learn how to document toggle proficiently.

This example of my continued journey to learn technology taught me one additional lesson: Embracing professional growth will not only best prepare you for any challenge that presents itself in the professional setting, but it will also serve as the best learn-by-example lesson for students.

KEY TAKEAWAYS

Always pursue professional growth opportunities to stay motivated and inspired.

- Identify areas of needed growth that will help you in times of crisis and in your everyday teaching activities.

- Choose which areas of growth to work on that tie directly to your professional or personal goals.
- Identify strategies and resources to work on these areas of growth.
- Identify specific ways your new growth expertise can improve your professional and personal lives.
- Explore new creative outlets for your new expertise.

LESSON 4

Toot Your Own Horn and Own Your Value

Teachers do extraordinary work in their classrooms that most times goes unnoticed and unrecognized. Lessons that are planned, prepped, and executed day after teaching day are met with student successes despite challenges presented by major crises, minor disruptions like students being taken out of academic classes for holiday concert rehearsals, or something as simple as the time of day a lesson is presented. Period 1 students are usually still sleepy. Period 4, which is right before lunch, has students drained from sitting for four hours straight, hungry, and more focused on food. Period 6, directly after lunch, has students running on over-the-top energy from their digested lunches and recess. And period 8, the last of the day, has students generally just spent or thinking about getting to practices, changing into gear, and making the team bus for that afternoon's game. Teachers and students alike get through these challenges, but who really sees teachers' hard work and successes?

Teaching is a solitary profession for the most part. We enter our classrooms at 7:00 a.m. and do not emerge until 3:00 p.m., spending the bulk of our day with our students. Teachers may comment to their team teachers if a lesson went extraordinarily well or not, but our lessons, and by extension our student triumphs, ultimately stay within our classroom walls. It is common for administrators to visit classrooms for five minutes or so when doing their daily walk-throughs, but how accurately can district and school leadership assess the effectiveness of a lesson or teacher in that short time frame? Or for that matter, even during a full-period formal observation, how accurate can these evaluations really be?

These questions loom even larger in times of crisis. For example, a colleague's formal observation was overshadowed by a "hold in place" while a medical emergency was addressed in the school. The students lost focus on their academic tasks, peppering the teacher with questions about what was happening, while the school administrator became more interested in evaluating how well the teacher was handling the crisis and the students. However, the evaluation methodology doesn't allow space to capture any skill set but the traditional classroom instruction and curriculum assessment. That means the teacher's evaluation score was artificially low due to the circumstances keeping the teacher from meeting the day's instructional criteria. The teacher had to lobby to get a new evaluation, which did happen in the end.

Grading Teachers

In my thirty-five years of teaching, I have had a continuous stream of district and school administrators. Over the past twenty-two years, I have had, on the district level, six school superintendents, three district curriculum directors, and four special education directors, and on the building level, eight principals and four assistant principals. These individuals basically judged my worth as a classroom teacher according to their "performance model" of choice. Though they consistently rated me "highly effective," as each serving administrator exited their position and a new hire was brought in, their professional opinions of me began to matter less and less.

Many years ago, during a professional development workshop on the new teacher performance tool used to evaluate pedagogical staff, the facilitator stated that school administrators would expect every teacher to work toward "fours" or "highly effective" every teaching period of every day. I raised my hand and turned that statement back to the facilitator, asking, "If admin expects fours from us, shouldn't we expect fours from them?" The audience of teachers smiled, and the facilitator didn't have an answer for me. While some administrators I've had have believed that our teaching staff consistently reached that goal of getting to fours, I've also had administrators who believed it was near impossible for teachers to reach the "highly effective" rating. What, then, is a teacher to think of this evaluation process?

Most importantly, and as this example shows, teachers must understand that the process of evaluating teachers is highly subjective, even with formal rating tools that require "evidence" to justify the ratings. This is why I do not give much weight to the professional opinions of my administrators. After thirty-five years in the classroom, no one defines my professional value other than myself, my students, their parents, and my colleagues.

The nature of the profession, however, is that teachers are evaluated. Teachers must be evaluated—in fact, all professionals must be evaluated—but the system isn't always fair, and those doing the evaluations aren't always up to the task.

All teachers have observation horror stories: the administrator who was late and missed half the lesson, the administrator who taught for all of three years in a non-content area and now evaluates high school advanced placement teachers, the administrator who didn't understand the math lesson but still had to evaluate how well the math teacher taught it and whether their students understood it. Crises, now part of classroom life, also show up in teacher observations. Unexpected events as minor as an unscheduled fire alarm going off or an anxious student having a panic attack during the observation class period disrupt the instruction and further tax a teacher's skill set. I myself was informally observed the very day I came back from bereavement leave after losing my father. I decided in the moment to just do the best I could, as sad and stressed as I was, and let my evaluation be what it would be.

When you combine those common observation issues with the low retention rate many schools have for keeping administrative staff, it's no wonder teachers have a hard time making "fours." Again, in the past nine years, I have had twelve different administrators evaluate my effectiveness, each with their own academic backgrounds, or not, and evaluation biases.

The most important piece of advice I can offer is to never allow an observation rating to define your worth as an educator. When I posted this advice on my InOurClassrooms Facebook page, I received over 3,300 "thumbs-up" and "love" reactions. Clearly, the inequities of teacher observations hit a unifying chord among nationwide educators. So how can we teachers fortify ourselves against this constant stream of judgments that can be harsh, misguided, sometimes completely baseless, and wrong? In short, how can we teachers recognize our own professional value in school organizations?

Own Your Value

Years ago, an administrator and I had a disagreement. They began their reprimand by saying, "You are an excellent educator and have value," to which I quickly replied, "You don't need to tell me I am an excellent educator. I *know* I am an excellent educator. No one tells me my value; I *know* my value." My words stopped them cold, and once the air was cleared, the issue was resolved. I walked out with my strong sense of self on full display.

Every successful classroom teacher knows their value, and they use it to help their students and themselves meet whatever challenges are presented. Teachers use this cultivated bravado to exude a strong presence to calm our students and bolster our own confidence levels, allowing us to feel we can handle any situation and lead in any crisis to a successful outcome. During the major crisis of COVID-19, many of us mired in our own stress-induced anxieties didn't even realize the accomplishments we had achieved beyond keeping our students occupied for short stints of time. This is why it is necessary to always keep your value in sight.

Remember, our goal here is to get into the habit of focusing less on the negative and more on the positive experiences in our classrooms.

To keep yourself rooted in your value, keep a paper or digital file of your work accomplishments, accolades, and letters of commendation. My suggestion is that every teacher—first-year rookie to twentieth-year expert—keep every personalized student and parent note and every positive student, parent, and administrator email. Keep each district posting on happenings in your classroom. Do not store these testimonials away; instead, buy a bulletin board and display them either in your classroom or in your home office or anyplace where you complete your schoolwork. My last suggestion is to read and reread these notes of appreciation often to remind you of and reinforce your own value as an educator. Review this collection often and with pride. Update your curriculum vitae regularly to reflect your new skill sets, coursework, degrees, and competencies.

Your Best Advocate—YOU!

How can teachers be recognized by others for the work we do? Teachers, we must be our own best public relations consultants showcasing our student achievements, which tie directly to our talents as curriculum developers and instructional practice experts. When we showcase our students in their learning moments, it allows administrators, colleagues, parents, and the larger school community to see inside our classrooms, and it allows our students to see their successes celebrated.

Showcasing student achievements accomplished during times of crisis is even more important than on a typical day, as it demonstrates student resilience and can motivate both student and teacher. As COVID-19 protocols were quietly being discontinued, school buildings had little extra room to store the vast pandemic-related supplies, including hundreds of clear plastic desk dividers. The leadership in my district announced a contest that invited teachers and students to come up with creative uses for the clear plastic. In my science classes, students dismantled the dividers and created model microscope slide specimens using the largest middle plastic section, card stock, markers, and paints. Students replicated human tissue cells, protists, and bacteria, to name a few. Models were put on display in the science wing, showcased in the district newsletter, and celebrated on the district's Facebook page. My students won second place for their creativity and science acumen.

Get Your Successes Seen—Self-Promotion

Teachers, we need to become comfortable in self-promotion, as it establishes our value within our school learning communities. Self-promotion is a nuanced skill, so as you begin, keep these guideposts in mind:

- Students' individual achievements and successes should be within the school organization's mission statement and strategic goals and plans as these drive district initiatives.

- Choose what specific achievements to promote wisely, and limit the promotion to once a month.
- Take pictures of your students in action, then write a short blurb of what the lesson is and what skills the students are practicing and mastering, then share with your district webmaster for social media postings.
- If you know your students are working on a culminating project or making class presentations, invite building and district leadership into your classroom for the event.
- Find and claim some wall space near your classroom to display student work and projects. Always complete the display with a write-up of what the student work shows and how it is connected to the curriculum.
- Always be aware of your own value, as it will keep you motivated, engaged, productive, and creative.[1]

Be Your Own Cheerleader

In the fall of 2020, teacher expectations for student engagement were high, and for the first time, I felt incredibly confident of my own tech proficiency. For one forty-eight-minute co-teach lesson, twenty-five online students engaged with my co-teach colleague and me "99+" separate times with questions and comments. In that split-second moment of glancing at the bottom of my computer screen and seeing that "99+," I knew that small data snapshot would duly impress my principal—not just in terms of student engagement, but more importantly *my ability and my co-teacher's* to engage twenty-five students over a hundred times during a fifty-minute Zoom science lesson.

When I shared my achievement of engaging 99+ students with my principal, he asked if I would speak to some colleagues about how to increase their student online engagement. ME!

Teachers, we must recognize our own professional value in our school organizations so other key stakeholders will as well. When we embrace and tout our expertise, talents, strengths, and value as educators, others will respect and value us.

Teachers are used to being behind a classroom door, so we may be uncomfortable self-publicizing our lessons, activities, and projects. As solitary professionals, however, we must begin to see the extraordinary work we do, document it, and publicize it. Teachers accomplish incredible successes every day in our classrooms—accomplishments that we must celebrate publicly if we are to be acknowledged.

Toot your own horn, teachers, to get the recognition you deserve, and your students will shine.

KEY TAKEAWAYS

Teachers must recognize and celebrate our own professional value.

- Have the mindset that you are your own best public relations consultant.
- Showcasing student achievements that tie directly to your talents as a curriculum developer and instructional practice expert allows administrators, colleagues, parents, and the larger school community to see inside your classroom, and it allows your students to see their successes celebrated.
- Use district media outlets to your advantage.
- Never allow an observation rating to define your worth as an educator.
- Keep your own celebratory file filled with personalized student and parent notes, media postings, administrator commendations, emails, and district postings on happenings in your classroom.

Part 2

UNSUNG ESSENTIAL WORKERS

During lunch period, the fire alarm sounded. Teachers knew this drill was unplanned since student drills were never during lunch periods. I sat at my desk for an extra minute, listening not to the fire alarm bells ringing but for the possible sounds of gunshots. Not a strange reaction for a teacher who has gone through school shooter training, including "a shooter may pull a fire alarm during lunch to do maximum bodily damage." Exiting the building, panicked students found and kept close to their on-edge teachers, asking, "Is this a planned drill?"

Teachers had to remain calm so our students would remain calm. The alarm, it turned out, was triggered by a panini press, which was a relief. However, the anxious moments stayed with many staff and students for the remainder of the school day.

Today's classroom teachers need to be prepared for any type of disruption or crisis. These can include lack of student focus and interest, chronic student absenteeism, excessive use of cell phones in classrooms, student emotional and mental health issues, school violence, and even teacher backlash.

At the height of the pandemic, teachers were revered as we showed up daily to keep our country's educational system up and running. And a lot has happened since then.

Come take a walk in our shoes, the unsung essential workers.

LESSON 5

Don't Get on the Circus Train

I always considered my public health degree and background an asset that I brought to my biology students. Teaching should look beyond an isolated concept to see its broader effects and consequences, and that is what public health strives to do—look out for the masses, not the individual. Teaching students the causes and consequences of a pandemic and living through one are both helped and hindered by a little bit of public health expertise.

Surprisingly, COVID-19 was not the first pandemic to make its way into my lesson planning. In the early 2000s,

I had to reassure my students that SARS was not and should not be a concern. Next was avian flu, though the 2007 H1N1 limited epidemics hit a bit closer to home. In 2011, I spent much time assuring my students that Ebola was not on its way from Africa to the United States East Coast. That was until an infected Sierra Leone citizen landed in Texas and died in an American hospital while infected American nurses and doctors were flown back from Africa to the United States for Ebola treatment. But as COVID-19 was rapidly spreading around the globe, it became clear very quickly that this pandemic would have consequences much closer to home.

Science Is Knowledge in the Face of Uncertainty

COVID-19 started innocuously enough. I remember first hearing about it in early December 2019; I read a snippet about a flu-like illness gripping a central region in China. Always wanting to keep abreast of all emerging health issues for my students, I researched the scant information available at the time and barely mentioned the illness to my students in an otherwise chock-full fifty-minute instructional period.

Over the course of that Christmas holiday break, nightly news broadcasts were mentioning this worsening viral illness more frequently. So much so that when we returned that first week in January, I presented the new emerging virus in a more constructive manner, SMART Board slides and all. Of course, I wince now, considering the virus propagated anti-Asian targeted violence, but I did present it as the "China flu" since in the field of virology or epidemiology, new viruses are often named after their place of origin. Lyme disease, for example, was named for where it was first detected, in Lyme, Connecticut. However, the best teachers learn alongside their students, and I, too, gained an early valuable lesson. In the future, this educator will only identify emerging viruses by their structure, not their place of origin.

Introducing this emerging virus to my students, I included pictures of the wet market presumed to be where the first case was transmitted in China's Wuhan Province. I went so far as to include a map to illustrate the almost eight thousand miles between Wuhan and lower Westchester County, New York, to ease my students' anxiety. Not being able to put much past my bright student virologists, they were astute enough to know that modern air travel could take a deadly virus from anywhere in the world and bring it to our own backyard in a matter of hours. My rudimentary lesson included whatever information about the virus was available. It was an emerging virus, never seen before in a human population, the symptoms being flu-like, and the virus possibly jumping from animal to human in the wet markets of Wuhan. My students peppered me with questions: "What animal is the host?" "How did it jump to the human?" "What are wet markets?" And of course, "Will it come here?"

As their science teacher, it was my job to answer as accurately as I could and to not cause unnecessary anxiety about a virus literally on the other side of the planet. I even reviewed all the other news-making viruses that made the covers of *Newsweek* and *Time* through the years—SARS, avian flu, MERS, H1N1, Ebola, and Zika—each touted by the media as the next pandemic simply to sell their magazines. The one pandemic we had studied in depth was the 1918 Spanish flu pandemic, which had just passed its one-hundredth anniversary mark. As an educator, I strongly believe that science must be understood within the context of history, so yes, the 1918 flu pandemic was an important part of our virus unit. But throughout every lesson, I stressed that the only antidote to fear is knowledge and reassured my students again and again that the Wuhan virus would surely be contained.

Throughout the month of January, news organizations steadily reported flu-like symptoms showing up in people in Italy. By February, Italy and much of Europe were under siege by the newly named COVID-19 virus—COVID-19 for *coronavirus disease*, which is named for the virus's crown-like shape of the outer protein capsid, the disease that results from infection, and the number 19 for the year it first appeared in a human population. My own son, a senior at Quinnipiac University in Hamden, Connecticut, sent me a text message on January 19 telling me he was going to an army surplus store to buy survival gear, to which I replied, "Don't be ridiculous."

By late January, early February, the numbers of those infected in Europe were staggering, and yet, in this country, the administration was not all that concerned—at least not publicly. Colleagues, family, friends, and students were all asking me the same question: Do we need to be worried? The public-health-trained-professional-turned-biology-teacher implored all who asked those questions to "not get on the circus train" but to keep informed and listen to public health officials for their advice.

By the middle of January, the virus had reached the shores of the West Coast, specifically Snohomish County, Washington, in the form of a thirty-five-year-old man who had recently returned from Wuhan Province and was diagnosed with the virus on January 19. I was not really surprised that COVID-19 had officially arrived in the US, what with the ease and speed of international travel. Within five days, there were travel-related confirmed cases in Illinois, California, and Arizona. It took only another four days for person-to-person transmission cases to begin being reported. By March 3, sixty cases of COVID-19 had been reported across Arizona, California, Florida, Georgia, Illinois, Massachusetts, New Hampshire, New York, Oregon, Rhode Island, Washington, and Wisconsin. Of the sixty COVID-19 infections officially detected, eleven were person-to-person spread, twenty-one were travel related, and twenty-eight were unknown.[1]

I may not have been surprised that COVID-19 was officially here, but I was very surprised at the rate the virus was spreading.

It was increasingly clear to me that COVID-19 had most probably been here in the Northeast for at least a few months, maybe as early as late November/early December, with increases in flu-like illnesses even in my own Westchester County. If an emerging virus is not on the radar of medical professionals, it simply goes undetected and is chalked up as another virus. This is what initially occurred when COVID-19 first showed up in my own local community hospital's emergency department, literally down the block from where I live.

Patient Zero was an attorney who lived in New Rochelle, New York, and worked in Manhattan, across from the transportation hub Grand Central Station. He was dubbed "Patient Zero," though many others were infected in the US before him, because he was the first confirmed COVID-19 case recorded in New York City. Patient Zero experienced a slight cough and then a slight fever, prompting him to visit his physician on February 26. His physician instructed him to go to the nearest emergency room, which was our local community hospital. Doctors there diagnosed him with mild flu. At that moment in time, there were no recorded cases of COVID-19 in New York City or the surrounding suburbs. However, within forty-eight hours, Patient Zero was on life support and transferred to a major hospital center in Manhattan. By March 2, a definitive diagnosis was made: COVID-19.[2]

By that first March weekend, New York Governor Andrew Cuomo had declared a state of emergency due to the coronavirus. By March 9, the state had 142 confirmed cases, with 98 being in Westchester County. Then on March 12, the governor implemented a containment zone with a one-mile radius in New Rochelle, temporarily closing houses of worship, schools, and other large gathering facilities for two weeks. National Guard troops arrived almost immediately.[3]

By mid-March, our local hospital became Ground Zero, tents went up for triage, and military personnel arrived daily in coach buses normally reserved for our local school trips. Medical personnel walking to the neighborhood bagel shop were in full hazmat gear. News images from Midtown Manhattan, less than twelve miles south, showed empty streets, triage tents erected in Central Park, and refrigerated trucks to serve as morgues because the numbers of infected and dying were increasing at staggering rates.

In those early pandemic days, as their science teacher, I had to keep my students calm. To achieve that, I had to tell them repeatedly that when you know the science behind viruses, not only do you begin to understand them, but the fear in them is also taken away. My students became public health officials. They knew the structure of viruses, the RNA component of COVID-19, and how viruses are transmitted, so they knew to wash their hands often, keep their hands away from their faces, and stay away from others when talking.

As their science educator, I knew I had to lead with facts and dispel fiction, which is difficult when dealing with an emerging virus. When we returned from winter break that January, and COVID-19 was a flu-like virus half a world away, I initially told all my students that "no one is getting on the circus train, no one is going to worry needlessly, no one is going to believe what is being said because virologists do not even know much about the virus." "Circus train" equates to mass hysteria. Science equates to facts, not fiction.

Once the governor shut down in-person learning for our school district and we went to remote learning, COVID-19 lessons continued to help my science students and their parents stay informed and minimize their natural anxiety. So many parents sent me email after email thanking me for keeping their children calm and informed as they recounted the daily COVID-19 science lessons during dinner. Of course, when we finally returned to school that next September, those former seventh graders, now eighth-grade students, would ask me in passing, "Ms. Richter, are we ever going to get off this circus train?!"

I gently reassured them that yes, life is now different from what we have experienced. I also framed our experiences in a historical context, just as we had learned about the 1918 pandemic. We were and would always be part of history as having experienced the 2020 pandemic.

The Relieving Role of Humor for Stress

When it comes to responding to adversities as a teacher, "do not forget humor," as Thomas L. shares. "Humor is a must in every crisis—in responding and in moving forward from it." Research behind the relieving role of humor for stress is well documented. Laughter allows the intake of oxygen-rich air, which stimulates your heart, lungs, and muscles and increases the endorphins that are released by your brain. Laughter dampens down your stress response and decreases your heart rate and blood pressure. Laughter stimulates blood circulation and naturally and quickly relaxes major muscle groups.[4] Nothing unifies the classroom teacher experience more than humor, as evidenced in the record-shattering Bored Teachers "The Struggle Is Real" comedy tour that has filled hundreds of theaters nationwide with over two hundred thousand teachers over the past three years.[5]

Big or Small, Know Your Crisis-Calming Bag of Tricks

The life of a classroom teacher is constantly filled with small disruptors and large-scale crises. How we react to these interruptions determines how quickly we can get back to the business of instruction. Fortifying yourself with knowledge can dispel fear and panic, keep you out of the mass hysteria swirling around you, and prevent you from getting on the circus train. Each one of us must also be aware of what will help reduce our stress and anxiety, so our students can bounce back successfully as well.

KEY TAKEAWAYS

Lead with knowledge in stressful classrooms.

- Keeping calm for yourself and your students is vital to the flow, structure, and tone of your every-day, every-period classroom environment.
- Rely on the experts to guide you through major crisis protocols and procedures.
- Carve out classroom time for stress-reducing strategies, including meditation, physical activities, and humor breaks.
- Speak to district leadership to include wellness professional development in future workshops.
- Fortifying yourself with knowledge will dispel the fear and hysteria for any crisis.

LESSON 6

Do No Harm

Throughout the two years of "pandemic teaching," our mantra was Do No Harm. Administrators repeated it often and loudly. New York City and its closest suburbs were hit hard by the pandemic—loss of lives, loss of jobs, loss of homes, loss of freedom, loss of social contact, loss of shared activities. The losses were traumatic, life changing, and seemingly endless. Our community was a mere twenty minutes from NYC, with many parents working there, so what was happening there rippled into our own bedroom community.

Our students were home, in their rooms, tied to screens all day and probably all night. Our most at-risk students were untethered to the stability of support staff, meals, friends, and teachers. Our objective in those early pandemic days and months was to show up online so our students still had connection to the outside world at a time when the world was in a state of shock.

Doing What Is Best for the Student—Always

Teachers will often say that our work is never boring, probably because no two days are ever the same, and in the higher grades, no two periods are ever the same for that matter. Each day brings new issues that often must be addressed before any learning can take place.

In my own experience, I have had students suddenly left homeless due to their apartment building burning down in the middle of the night, students repeatedly falling asleep in class due to baby siblings keeping the whole family awake throughout the night, and students becoming so severely stressed due to college application deadlines or sitting for SAT exams that they simply shut down. Students are exposed to family problems and losses, health issues, social media influences, peer issues, and school safety fears. Today's students are confronted with many different types of crises—some that have quick fixes and others that require much time and professional resources. No matter if a crisis affects a single student or the entire school body, doing what is best for the student—always—is what is truly meant by doing no harm.

Anyone who works in the field of education knows being a kid today is tough. The concerns our students face today are unprecedented, and often academic responsibilities are last on their list of priorities. As their teachers, we understand our students and always do what is best for them, even on occasion removing academic stress as they grapple with other more serious concerns.

In those initial COVID-19 lockdown months, academic rigor was, of course, thrown out the window. June 2020 saw New York state cancel all end-of-year content exams, called Regents exams, and my school district, as most, likewise canceled final exams as well. The last burden we wanted to add to our students' and their families' lives was academic pressure. Parents were thankful for the removal of academic pressure, and students quickly embraced the idea as well.

The physical, emotional, and mental health of our students became paramount, and the district made the choice of not even counting last-quarter grades in yearly final grade averages. Teachers were instructed to be "flexible" and tread lightly in assigning and grading classwork. Most teachers understood and agreed with the district's decision. How could we not, with most of us experiencing our own family issues—spouse job losses, our own children Zooming into their classes alongside us on the living room couch, and our high school seniors losing their proms, award ceremonies, and graduations and not even knowing if they would be going off to their chosen colleges in a few months. Living through the raging days of the COVID-19 pandemic, without a doubt, gave us, the teachers, permission to be imperfect, exhausted, overwhelmed, and lenient on the number, type, scope, and grading of assignments.

Changing priorities during a global crisis makes perfect sense. But what criteria do we use for lesser crises that our students experience, and who creates those criteria? I will argue that for crises that affect individual students, the teacher has the decision-making power to extend academic deadlines, reduce academic workloads, modify academic assignments, and decide which assignments a student can be exempted from. Teachers must let teacher-colleagues, guidance counselors, administration, and parents know, but it is the right of the academic teacher to make these adjustments to best serve their students. In making these accommodations, however, teachers must also have a responsible plan for gradually bringing the student back to normal academic expectations.

Classroom teachers make these kinds of decisions often. Let us say I had a student who broke their leg while on a skiing trip. The student would be out from school for close to three months due to multiple surgeries and rehab stints. This student would be expected to take a state Regents exam at the end of the school year—a mere month after returning to school. I know I would have to drastically modify the biology curriculum, keeping in mind limited teaching time and reliance on home study provided by a tutor, so I would adjust my lessons to focus only on key concepts tailored to the Regents exam.

School Is for More Than Just Academics—Especially in a Crisis

For those on the outside looking in, schools are simply places for learning academics—reading, writing, and arithmetic—but schools are so much more. Schools are places where peer relationships develop and flourish, where teachers become mentors and allies, where meals are shared, where dreams are supported, and where joy and fun are encouraged.

In those first few pandemic months, our students had every right to have little focus or even care to edit their American history essays, study for their math test, or finish and submit that book response while their parents were losing jobs or FaceTiming with nurses caring for their elderly grandparents in area hospitals stricken with COVID-19. Many days during virtual class time, students just needed to be connected to others. On those days, we allowed students to be silly, make jokes, show us their pets, even pick up their baby siblings for a cameo. Often, our students just wanted to hear us, their teachers, tell them everything was eventually going to be "back to normal," "fine," and even "better than fine."

Though COVID-19 was such an unusual experience, we still learned important takeaways for the role of teachers in any crisis. Teachers, usually the academic enforcer, in a crisis now take on the role of comforter. Teachers encourage students to unplug from their devices, be physically active, get out into nature, do what they like to do, and above all be kind and gentle with themselves. Silliness, laughter, and fun have a place in the classroom to momentarily alleviate stress and to strengthen student–teacher bonds.

Looking Back Prepares for the Future

While many students continued to be focused learners and do their best, there were just as many who had tremendous difficulty with the transition to online learning during COVID-19. Students refused to turn on their Chromebook cameras or attended virtual school while in their pajamas in bed with their blankets pulled up to their chins. Students were more interested in engaging with their peers in Google Classroom Chats than answering questions from their teachers. For a few, assignments stopped being completed and turned in at all.

Academic grade averages fell swiftly and, in some cases, substantially between April and June 2020. Some students stopped logging on to their Chromebooks altogether, and those were the students we worried about most. In the absence of a pandemic, home visits would have immediately been scheduled for our at-risk students, but health protocols made this impossible. For us teachers and school guidance staff, this was the most frustrating: not being able to physically see and help our students.

Though the COVID-19 crisis has passed, we still need to look back, identify protocol gaps, and fix them for future crises. How will we physically reach at-risk students? What can we do to ensure students log on during virtual class? How do we keep students vested in the learning process during any type of crisis? Federal, state, and local educational stakeholders need to look hard at these questions and develop plans before we need to implement them on a large scale. But official plans and protocols, which come from the top down, take time. During a crisis, teachers immediately need suggestions and strategies to keep their students vested, from colleagues and students alike. I know if my instruction had to revert to online lessons, I would ask the students how the lessons should be framed, which activities to keep, and which to discard. I would also start online teacher communities seeking others' digital instructional best practices that I could possibly use. I certainly would lean into more student-group interaction types of instructional activities.

Priorities Are Never Set in Stone

In late April 2020, *The New York Times* published an article focused on the stressors of academic pressure during a pandemic. I posted a response that was published as a *NYT* Readers Pick where I commiserated with the struggles parents were going through, being a teacher and mother myself, and encouraged parents and students to unplug when necessary and not stress over schoolwork but view it more as a means to stay positively occupied.[1]

My words resonated with 475 *New York Times* subscribers. Academic grades took the right place on the priority list—last place—while we were navigating a once-in-a-hundred-years pandemic. Crises are part of a teacher's regular school day. In responding to crises, priorities should not be guided by what has always been done but rather what is best for our students, their families, and ourselves.

KEY TAKEAWAYS

In the face of a crisis, always remember to do no additional harm, prioritizing empathy and student well-being.

- Mental, emotional, and physical health of our students take precedence.
- Be flexible in academic requirements for students in crisis.
- Prioritize student self-care and connecting with others.
- Encourage students to unplug from their devices and the news and plug into silliness and fun instead.
- Teachers must always lead with empathy.

LESSON 7

Building Resilience

In September 2020, schools were back in session, and the school philosophy of Do No Harm was still fully in effect, as it should have been. Class periods, normally forty-eight minutes and now over ninety minutes, were twice as long to avoid movement among students and to limit exposure in case a student or teacher had COVID-19. Students were on a schedule where half the student body were physically in the school building, while the other half of their peers were at home, logged on to their computers. As it was easier to focus on the students in front of us, our kids at home got even less of their teachers' attentions. Teachers were still assigning scant academic work, students were still not taking schoolwork seriously, and parents were still expecting their children's assigned work to be at a minimum and graded leniently.

In our school district, a far greater threat in late fall/early winter was the non-COVID-19 yearly flu, which ran rampant throughout all grades. At one point, nearly two-thirds of our students were out on any given day. The rolling absences kept students out for anywhere from four to eight days, and, again, much discussion was had about academic accountability. Many teachers, having learned a valuable lesson through the pandemic, marked missed work as *exempt* so as to not add pressure to still-anxious students and parents. Once again, teachers, support staff, and administrators agreed to loosen academic accountability until the flu virus was under control.

COVID-19 Wreaking Havoc on Education

Five years out from the COVID-19 crisis, research confirms what administrators, teachers, students, and parents have intuitively known since those early 2020 school shutdowns: COVID-19 wreaked havoc on our educational system and its stakeholders. Universally, experts in multiple fields agree that schools stayed closed for far too long, transitioning to virtual learning was both distracting and ineffective, student absences soared, mental and emotional issues surfaced, and teacher shortages skyrocketed, all combining in a severe loss of instructional time resulting in plummeting reading and math competencies for K–12 learners.[1]

Of course, hindsight is twenty-twenty. This strategy of Do No Harm made sense then. My principal at the time repeatedly said, "This is our first pandemic," but even us frontline teachers had no inkling of its impact moving forward.[2]

Traveling the Road to Recovery While It's Being Built

When we returned in January 2021 following the flu outbreak, marking a year since the crisis onset, school life was not much better. Students were still not completing and turning in assignments on time and had little vested interest in their grades, and behaviors both in the classroom and in Zoom classes were markedly worse. Classroom teachers still hesitated to contact parents because we had no idea what stressors were being experienced by individual families or even what student homelife looked like anymore. School support staff and administrators continued to emphasize that teachers had to follow Do No Harm, which parents agreed with and were especially thankful for. A few parents, however, continued to equate Do No Harm with top grades for little work completed by their children. As we headed into the spring of 2021, the New York State Department of Education canceled state English language arts and math exams for grades 3–8 and Regents exams for grades 8–12 for a second year straight, while teachers were concerned with rising and solidifying student academic apathy and increased and chronic absenteeism, which was translating into few, if any, gains in academic benchmarks.

By the start of the following September 2021 school year, all pandemic restrictions had been lifted, masks were being taken off, plexiglass desk shields were dismantled, and lunch tables buzzed with student chatter. Do No Harm, too, should have been replaced with increased student expectations and academic rigor, but it was not.

As we rang in January 2022, now two years out from the initial lockdowns, maintaining pre-pandemic student attendance rates, appropriate student behavior, and rigorous academic expectations were difficult at best. Student behavior issues continued to disrupt classroom learning environments, student absences became the norm, and student failures kept rising due to the lack of being present in class and completing assignments. As the year hobbled to the finish line that June, teachers had experienced as stressful a year as the initial pandemic year. Teachers were exhausted from the lack of student interest, motivation, and effort and the general malaise students exhibited.

The 2022–23 and 2023–24 school years saw school

routines and academic expectations slowly returning to pre-pandemic days, and rigor was officially back, as were state tests. Even as 2024 moved into 2025, a few students and their parents still looked for assignment extensions and grade inflation, in part because of the disruptions and crises that still encroach on our classrooms.

Finding the Right Time to Reinstate Rigor

"Students Lost One-Third of a School Year to Pandemic, Study Finds," read the January 30, 2023, *New York Times* headline. It is true the disruption in normal school instruction led to disruptions in meeting learning benchmarks, but without a doubt, the post-pandemic lag in returning to school routines and expectations—and yes, academic rigor—delayed student progress even more so. Well into 2023, a few students and parents continued to push back against academic rigor as student absences were still high, and waves of illness continued to roil through students and staff alike. Parents were still expecting leniency for these absences and exceptions for disruptive student behaviors and advocating for high grades for subpar work, late work, and even work not done at all.

Teachers across the country experienced many of the same negative consequences in the classroom. Maddy, a guidance counselor, laments, "It seems as if young people have no idea what academic responsibility and accountability means anymore."

Larry, a district-wide staff developer, adds, "The pandemic may have ended, but teachers still report students and their parents who are looking for top grades without any student effort or parent oversight put in."

Charmaine, a middle school honors teacher, has never been more frustrated in her twenty-seven-year teaching career than now. "Students come to school in their pajamas, literally rolling right out of bed, without their review packets so ill prepared for the day's work, more focused on their cell phone screens than on the lesson, never asking clarifying questions or seeking me out during my office hours, and only when they do poorly on their assessments do they ask for extra credit for higher grades."

Joann, a high school principal, feels her teachers' frustrations. "School administration receives tremendous pushback from parents as we try to build back academic, behavioral, and social expectations of their children in the school environment."

Teachers on the front lines of academia started asking, "When does the policy of Do No Harm become harmful for all involved parties?"

We know what COVID-19, as a major crisis, has done to education. Now is the time to focus on the current crises of school violence, rising debilitating teen anxiety disorders, and the absence of resilience in our youth and develop strategies to prevent future crises from having the same devastating effects on our students.

The Path Forward

One of the major concerns that COVID-19 exposed was a lack of resiliency in students. During the crisis, and now years after, students did not have the capacity to recover from the severe disruptions the crisis caused. Students were excused from all school-related responsibilities, which, in hindsight, prevented them from building resiliency and moving forward.

What our COVID-19 experience has proven is that for future crises, it will be important to foster resiliency by reinstating pre-pandemic school and classroom routines as well as classroom expectations and academic rigor sooner, not later. Students must show up every day on time and ready to work. Student assignments must be done for correctness and not just completeness, and students must meet assignment deadlines or face academic penalties. Students must be active learners and be respectful learning-community citizens. In fact, key to this will be making parents and students aware of routines and expectations and keeping them in place during crises instead of removing them or relaxing them.

Resiliency is a necessary skill for life's daily challenges, and perhaps we did not do our students any favors by excusing them from facing at least some of those challenges.

COVID-19's Learning Toll Affected More Than Just Grades

Although school routines returned to pre-pandemic "normal," the effects of the virus lockdown were evident in student psyches. State tests showed significant proficiency gaps in student reading and math levels, and writing skills were also lacking, as were critical thinking, organizational skills, and executive functioning skills.[3] Students could be described as "helpless,""clueless," and some even "defeated" in figuring out how to meet academic challenges once again. As teachers, we heard student laments of "I don't remember how to do this," "I can't do this," "I will never be good at this again," "I try, but nothing works," and "I studied the material, but I still don't get it." Emerging from the pandemic, student mindsets had shifted to a "stuck" and "fixed" position, and it fell to teachers to show students how to get unstuck.

The view one has of oneself has the most direct effect on the type of success that person will have in their own life. One view people have is that their abilities are set in cement and can never develop further to any significant degree. This mindset, often referred to as a "fixed" mindset, can be frustrating at best and debilitating at worst if the individual believes they can never get any better or smarter no matter the time or effort they put into a task.

There are others, however, who view their abilities as continuously developing through effort, through use of specific strategies, and by surrounding themselves with others who support their growth. This type of mindset—a growth mindset—intrinsically allows individuals to feel comfortable with their current situation, as they know they can change it for the better through personal and professional development.

The Growth Mindset Solution

In the twenty-first century, there has been a proliferation of research on growth mindset and its integration into the educational setting and intrinsic motivation in learning driven by the decades-long work of Carol Dweck. *Growth mindset* is defined as a belief that intelligence is improvable. Students with a growth mindset are likely to learn by a mastery approach, with teachers setting practice goals in place that lead to skill and content-mastery acquisition over time. A mastery approach encourages students to embrace challenges and put effort into learning. For instance, growth-minded individuals perceive task setbacks as a necessary part of the learning process, and they "bounce back" by increasing their motivational effort.[4]

Much of Dweck's research has relied on qualitative approaches for assessing students' self-reports. One recent study on elementary school students showed that leveraging an online educational game with in-game rewards can promote a growth mindset in low-performing students by directly incentivizing effort and encouraging persistence.[5] Yet developments in brain science research are paving the way for and stressing the importance of developing quantitative research to support our understanding of growth mindsets in the classroom. Neuroscientific research in education shows learners with growth mindsets tend to embrace lifelong learning and the joy of incremental personal growth.[6]

As teachers, how do we encourage a growth mindset so our students can have their own best outcomes? Our primary role in our classrooms is to support students as they seek knowledge through collaboration, research, experimentation, and critical thinking. We find ways to tap into our students' natural curiosity. We provide engaging and fun learning opportunities to encourage our students to develop a lifelong appreciation for learning. We, as change agents, model strategies to face challenges, deal with problems, and grow from each experience—both positive and negative. We believe that ability, talent, and intelligence can grow with exposure and practice. We set high academic standards for our students, and within nurturing learning communities, we provide the strategies and practice to meet those standards. We challenge our students every day so they will have the ability to meet any challenge life throws at them.

During the COVID-19 crisis and beyond, the Do No Harm policy reinforced a fixed mindset among our youth. Academic, behavioral, and social expectations for students were at a minimum while they still were able to achieve good grades. Students saw absolutely no need to put in any work for the academic grades they were simply being given. After two years, when expectations were slowly reinstated, students still resisted attending school, completing work, turning work in, and meeting academic standards for quality work. Even four years later, it was still a struggle, at times, for students to see their own abilities and to use strategies to reach those abilities. A student may not review or study for a unit test, and when they receive a low grade, they ask for test corrections to earn points back. When the student discovers this is not an option, they do not react well and do not see what strategies will help them succeed.

This is the true importance of instilling a growth mindset in students, especially in the shadow of COVID-19 or any life disruptor. A student must believe they can learn and grow in order to build resilience. When my own students fall into these moments of defeat, I point to a classroom wall that has one simple word spelled out in orange letters that measure two feet high: *YET*.

"You can't do this YET."

"You are not quite good at this skill YET."

"You don't understand the content YET."

Yet is a powerful word because it lets the students know that they will get there, that they can grow, learn, and succeed.

The Secret Ingredient to Crisis Management

For all students to meet our expectations, teachers must infuse a growth mindset in the classroom so our students can carry it with them for life.

There are moments when we are no longer in control of life as we know it, turning us upside down and inside out, having us question our abilities, talents, and even intelligence. Those out-of-control moments do not come with an instruction booklet or even a start and end time. A growth mindset can have the most direct positive effect on navigating those unsettling experiences and set us on a successful life path. A growth mindset reassures us that no matter what comes our way, we can successfully meet the challenge.

Teachers can help students bounce back from crises by returning to norms as quickly as possible. Teachers must prioritize and hold students accountable for academic, behavioral, and social expectations. Concurrently, teachers must model and nurture growth mindsets in our students, as this builds resilience. Parents are our partners in their children's education, and as such, parents must be made aware of a school district's expectations for acceptable behaviors, academic rigor, and consequences for not meeting those standards. Parents' support of these policies is crucial for their children's growth and resilience.

KEY TAKEAWAYS

Maintaining routines, meeting expectations, and having a growth mindset allow us to withstand and recover from the effects of crises.

- School and classroom routines and expectations must be maintained through a crisis.
- Academic rigor should be reinstated and maintained as quickly as possible after a crisis.
- A growth mindset validates one's ability to learn, grow, and succeed.
- Meeting academic, behavioral, and social expectations builds resilience.
- Resilience gives students the ability to withstand and recover faster from crises.

LESSON 8

Put Down Those Devices

A few weeks ago, I walked into another teacher's classroom to hand her some papers she had left in mine. I heard her sternly telling an eighth grader to put his phone away and take his seat again. I looked to the left of where I was standing, and, sure enough, the eighth grader was holding up his hand to his teacher's face while he continued trying to punch in a phone number. Being a senior teacher, whose responsibility it is to assist during teaching disruptions, I was not having any insubordinate behavior. I told him to hand me the phone, which he eventually did.

On our way down to the assistant principal's office, where I intended to hand over both the phone and the student, I asked the student what he thought he was doing. He simply stated he was trying to call his mom. The young man saw no issue with making a call in the middle of class while the teacher was instructing. As our school does have a no-cell-phone policy, the phone was held until his mom came to pick it up, and the student served a two-day lunch detention in the assistant principal's office.

Juxtapose this incident with what occurred in my classroom. A seventh grader arrived visibly upset and immediately asked if they could go to the office to call their mom. I asked the student to step into the hallway for a moment, so I could assess the situation in private. My student explained that they had left their lunch at home, had no money to buy lunch, and needed to call their mom so she could drop off the lunch. I made the decision to allow the student to retrieve their cell phone from their locker and call their mom in the hallway with me. By allowing the student to call immediately, the mom would have some extra time to bring the child's lunch to school before the lunch period, and the student would not lose any instructional time. Once the student reached their mom, they quickly calmed down, knowing she was on the way and they could now focus on the lesson.

Cell phones have become a hot-button issue in schools, specifically in classrooms, but the solution to this problem is not simple or clear cut.

The Problems with Cell Phones

How do cell phones interfere with student success? The research is extensive and strongly suggests that allowing phones in the classroom—whether out in full view, tucked in a pocket, or even seemingly safely put away in a book bag—gives students endless opportunities to text friends and family, watch movies, scroll TikTok, listen to music, or even shop online, which all negatively impact student focus.[1]

The mere presence of a cell phone undercuts student learning, retention of content and skills, task completion, enjoyment of learning tasks, and overall student test performance. "Michael Rich, an associate professor of pediatrics at Harvard Medical School and an associate professor of social and behavioral sciences at the Harvard T.H. Chan School of Public Health, says that phones and school don't mix: Students can't meaningfully absorb information while also texting, scrolling, or watching YouTube videos. 'The human brain is incapable of thinking more than one thing at a time,' he said. 'And so what we think of as multitasking is actually rapid-switch-tasking. And the problem with that is that switch-tasking may cover a lot of ground in terms of different subjects, but it doesn't go deeply into any of them.'"[2]

The New York Times went right to the source and asked teenagers what they thought about schools banning cell phones. The reactions were mixed. Many students brought up the same reasons they wanted access to their phones during the day: to listen to music, to contact their parents, and to do their schoolwork. But many recognized the need for some boundaries around phone use, with several supporting an outright ban.[3]

As classroom teachers, we do not need research to bear out our own observational data collected over the past four years with increased student cell phone use. Academically, students have *very* slowly been gaining back content and skill mastery. Students work slower, need tremendous teacher support for task completion, and request assignment extensions, and their student work is far below what is to be expected. We teachers have also seen substantial decreases in teacher-to-student social cues, peer-to-peer social cues, student oratory skills, and body language awareness. Social relationships have also been negatively impacted by the presence of cell phones in classrooms. The verified research, classroom teachers, and experts on the science of learning are all calling for a ban on cell phone use by students in schools. The question that must be examined, however, is whether a total cell phone ban is the right call or not.

Cell Phone Bans—the Solution or Worsening the Problem?

Before the 2019–2020 school year, 77 percent of US schools had moved or were actively working through their local school boards to ban cell phones for nonacademic use.[4]

In December 2019, who could have fathomed that in a mere two months, a pandemic would completely shut down the country, including the thousands of local school districts, forcing us into complete isolation without the benefit of extended family, friends, colleagues, jobs, schools, celebrations, and leisure activities? Our only communication lifeline to the outside world was our cell phones. For more than a year, while in social isolation, young people were able to choose when and how to use their cell phones. They used them throughout the "school day" while sitting in front of computer screens. They used them for entertainment, for information, and, perhaps most importantly, for social and emotional connections. When our students returned to in-person learning, they brought with them the one device that helped them survive their most trying days and nights: their cell phones. And now they were being asked to leave their primary source of comfort and connection in lockers, tucked away in backpacks, and even at home.

Our students most certainly have academic gaps and interpersonal skill delays, but is a complete ban of cell phones in schools going to reverse these trends? Without cell phone distractions, students may well focus better, leading to closing learning gaps. Without cell phone distractions, students may well start having more frequent interactions with peers, leading to authentic social and emotional connections.

While these scenarios do support the belief that cell phone bans are the solution to the problems left behind by the COVID-19 crisis, we also have to consider whether a ban could worsen student issues. Recently, while I was in a teaching period, I remembered my own cell phone, there on my desk, was not silenced. I apologized for stopping instruction to adjust my phone settings, and as I did, one of my students said out loud, "Ms. R., there is a cell phone ban in this school. How come your phone is out on your desk, but we can't have ours even in our backpacks?"

I responded jokingly, "When you have multiple degrees and sit at the teacher's desk, you, too, can have your cell phone out."

I have given some serious thought to my flippant response and see the inequity my student pointed out. I keep my cell phone handy in case there is a family emergency, my grown children need to contact me, or I want to check my emails or the news. My cell phone, like for my students, is my connection to the outside world during my eight-hour workday. This tech device provides information, entertainment, and, yes, comfort. If I did not have access to my cell phone, I would be a wreck, unable to concentrate or do my best work—and I am an adult. Can you imagine how difficult it is for students to not have their devices with them? How about the students who are suffering from extreme anxiety and depression? For those students, simply coming to school is an incredible feat of emotional and physical strength, and then add to that not having a connection to home by not having their cell phone? Parents are also not in favor of cell phone bans simply because they want to know they can reach their child in an emergency. A cell phone ban could easily make student issues much worse.

The prime objective of schools is to foster conducive learning environments, but in the age of cell phone technology, schools need to also develop usage policies that are humane and respectful for student users, as well as informative on the effects cell phones have on learning and their responsible use in schools. Therefore, a total cell phone ban may not be the most reasonable, or even doable, option. Instead, the better solution may be to teach students how to use them responsibly and provide spaces for them to be used and spaces free from them.[5]

Get Input from Those on the Ground for Policy

Emergencies and disasters take many different forms. Imagine what teachers, students, and school staff experienced during the late morning on April 5, 2024, in

Westchester County, New York, when we felt the building shake, accompanied by a deep growl coming from beneath our feet. Light fixtures swayed high above us as the shaking continued for over a minute as an unprecedented 4.7-magnitude earthquake struck.

Teacher reactions were mixed. Science teachers quickly realized this acute onset emergency and took students out of the classrooms and into the hallways, ready to evacuate. Other pedagogical staff, even after realizing they were experiencing an earthquake, stayed in the classrooms, not knowing any safety procedures to follow. When the shaking stopped and the earthquake was confirmed, administrators took the science teachers to task for "creating their own emergency protocols." Yet the science teachers were the experts for this sudden onset emergency. We knew what to do to keep our students safe.

Emergency protocols do not always need to come from the top down in an organization. Emergency protocols should come from those with knowledge and expertise in the specific emergency. Science teachers knew the best protocol during an earthquake was to evacuate a shaking classroom, where glassware, dangerous chemicals, and heavy equipment can seriously injure students if they stay put. As horrific as it is to even think about school shootings, even those protocols have changed over the past twenty-five years. For years, the standard protocol was always lockdown and shelter in place until police arrived. Teachers and students are now advised to run and evacuate if you can, use anything and everything to blockade yourself and your students inside a classroom, do not simply lock the door, and even fight the intruders if possible. These protocol changes arose from faculty, staff, students, and law enforcement officials who had experienced school shootings firsthand.

All school protocols must have room for specific situational conditions. Really, every situation that has standardized protocols must make room for other "best judgment" decisions, including cell phones in schools.

Cell Phones in an Anxiety-Filled Era

Teachers know COVID-19 created dramatic increases in the rate of anxiety problems and social, emotional, and mental health issues among children and adolescents in our classrooms. Many students feel less anxious having access to a phone (really, access to their parents), and parents feel more secure knowing they have a constant connection to their children. More than three-quarters of parents surveyed whose children have cell phones said they want their children to carry cell phones on their person throughout the school day. The primary reason? Parents want their kids to have cell phones at school so they can reach them in an emergency.[6]

While it's understandable that parents and students want constant access to cell phones in the case of emergencies, this can also lead to the issue of students' overreliance on parents for problems that aren't true emergencies. For these suffering adolescents, having a cell phone tucked in a hoodie pocket or book bag provides them with avenues for immediate communication for those school-induced stressors—receiving a lower-than-usual test grade, finding out they were not invited to *that* party, seeing a post or video involving themselves, or even being able to "report" their teacher for not calling on them at all or for unknowingly embarrassing them during the class period. We have all had students who are not able to cope ask to use the restroom and instead call their parents to cry, vent, or ask for parent intervention—now! It is not unusual for the parent to have already called the school principal to fix their child's issue even before the student has returned to our classroom.

On the surface, cell phones in the hands of students throughout their school day may seem to help, when in fact, they may be interfering with a student's ability to navigate their own experiences. By having access to their cell phones during their school day, students rely on their parents to run interference for them and fix each negative encounter, uncomfortable incident, and perceived slight.

If this continues unchecked, how will current middle and high schoolers ever learn to cope with disappointment? If parents are always the go-to problem solvers, how will our current generation of students ever learn how to be their own problem solvers? Many schools enlist their PTA organizations to sponsor parent workshops on student cell phone use in schools with emphasis on just this issue. Parents appreciate hearing from child experts on when and how they should get involved when it comes to their children's school and friend problems.

Technology Has Its Place, but It's Hard to Keep It There

Many teachers have students use their cell phones as an additional learning device in the classroom. Students can quickly access sites for polls, research, even data points. Of course, once the phone is out and students are tapping away, they tend to use the device for their own purposes. This behavior is not even limited to students. At a recent professional development session, teachers were told to leave their phones out to access a poll-taking site, which we did—between checking our own personal emails, digital news, and the like.

Yes, even teachers can be distracted by their own phones when not fully engaged in the lesson being presented. Bottom line is that for student and teacher alike, phone technology is addictive. Teachers are competing with a daunting tech foe for student attention. If our students are going to their phones, what is that saying about our learning activities, and how are we engaging our own students? Again, are we as teachers blaming the technology without taking a closer look at our own methodologies?

Get Clarity on the Real Problem

Perhaps too much attention is focused on the actual technology. Maybe the focus and targeted interventions should be on how and why some students use their cell phones consistently throughout the school day instead of focusing on academics or developing quality peer relationships.

Teachers, we see myriads of negative effects of having cell phones in the class, which is backed up by current research. We want our students to put down those devices so they can focus on the learning tasks at hand, make eye contact with their lab partner, converse in complete sentences within their reading circle group, or try to handle an issue on their own or turn to a teacher, a guidance counselor, even a friend before dialing home. Teachers must advocate for less cell phone usage by students in schools, as research shows cell phones interfere with student academic success.

But advocating for less cell phone usage should not necessarily mean a ban of cell phones in schools. Despite the negative aspects, teachers also see the value of students having cell phones for comfort, connection, and emergency situations. Teachers, heed this call to action. We must be involved in the cell-phone-ban decision-making process and help shape the policy, as our students' needs and successes depend upon it.

KEY TAKEAWAYS

Cell phones in classrooms are necessary but distracting.

- Research strongly suggests phones in the classroom negatively impact:
    - » student focus, learning, and retention of content and skills
    - » student decision-making skills
    - » student independence
- Cell phone bans are not the answer.
    - » Many students feel less anxious having access to a phone.
    - » Parents feel more secure knowing they have a constant connection.

LESSON 9

Let Your Voice Be Heard

When I was in my midtwenties and working in public health, I tagged along as the president of the hospital where I was working was giving his administrative team a tour of the new hospital addition. He showed off the new auditorium and asked us, his audience of underlings, what we thought of the heavy, dark-crimson stage curtains. The group of experienced and long-standing employees responded, "Looks good."

Without missing a beat, I offered my opinion. "The curtains are too heavy a material. And crimson red. Really?

The color of blood for an event space in a hospital? You should have gone with a lighter-weight material and a more soothing color palette."

My colleagues literally stepped a few inches away from me as my new boss stepped closer. He looked me straight in the eye and told me he had chosen those curtains and color himself and asked whether it was wise for me as the newest hire to speak up. I looked him straight in the eye and simply said, "You asked for my opinion, and I gave you my opinion." With that exchange, the hospital president knew he had an independent thinker who was not intimidated to use her voice. In that moment, I gained his respect and was often sought out for my candid opinions.

When I transitioned into teaching, I went from being "management" to "labor" and was carefully evaluated throughout my three-year probationary period by school and district leaders. Normally, school union leadership will strongly advise untenured teachers to lay low, not speak up, not voice opinions, and not take part in school decision-making. Tenure or no tenure, my voice was always strong, listened to, and respected.

Finding Your Teacher Voice

How can teachers express their ideas and opinions? Your voice is one of the most valuable parts of your being. Your voice allows you to communicate *your* feelings, *your* opinions, *your* ideas, and truths as *you* see them. To see the value in your individual voice, understand that there are millions of individuals who can *speak* but do not have a *voice*. The very young, the elderly, the poor, and the oppressed are the most disenfranchised groups, often lacking both individual and collective voices.

As teachers, we are experts in using our voices. Primarily, we use our voices to convey daily instruction with authority. Teacher voices encourage, motivate, and praise students with enthusiasm. Our voices celebrate student successes with excitement. We also use our voices to advocate on behalf of our students with determination. Teacher voices are heard individually and collectively.

Teachers Are Not the Villains

As illustrated in Dana Goldstein's detailed investigation into the history of teaching in America in her book, *The Teacher Wars*, compulsory education laws did not go into effect until the 1920s in America, and it wasn't until the 1940s that most children started graduating from high school, when there was a building boom for secondary schools. Teachers throughout the late 1800s to 1980s were highly respected professionals, mostly because they had the formal education other Americans did not. Teachers were preparing youth for jobs and professions not available to their immigrant parents and to make America into the economic powerhouse it was to become. Teachers, primarily women, chose to forgo their own families to focus on other people's children. Teachers were revered. Teachers were valued. Teaching as a profession was respected.[1]

The primary role of the teacher over the past 140 years has basically stayed the same—to academically prepare our youth for entering the workforce so that our nation can be economically competitive. Teachers are charged with developing students into critical thinkers and problem solvers with reading and math proficiency. Yet, over the past twenty-plus years, teachers have come under fire from the very stakeholders who used to be our fervent supporters.

Teachers have often been blamed for the failings of public education because we are the ones standing in the classroom. Being the most accessible and visible, even while providing the state-mandated curriculum via district-approved instructional practices, the classroom teacher is the easiest target for the deficiencies in the education system.

However, as teachers, we have a lot of stakeholders to account to, including state education departments, district and school administration, elected school board officials, colleagues, students, and parents. Since 2002, with the passage of No Child Left Behind legislation, the federal government has played a larger role in what teachers do in their individualized classrooms, spread out over the nearly fourteen thousand school districts in America today.

To blame teachers for the failings of our public education system is misguided at best and self-defeating at worst. Teachers have little to no power in the grand educational system within which we work. State education departments provide teachers with the K–12 content-learning standards we will be using to instruct our students. School districts inform teachers of the course loads we will be teaching for any given school year based on the professional certifications teachers hold. School administration directs their pedagogical staff to use set instructional practices to convey content and assessments. Teachers are assessed informally and formally to ensure content and instruction are within state and district guidelines.

To believe that teachers have independent control over curriculum, instruction, and assessment is misguided. Teachers have little to no voice in setting curriculum, instructing students, and assessing students, and with little to no voice, there is little to no power.

And Then Came COVID-19

When COVID-19 disrupted and upended life as we all knew it, as businesses shut down, as commerce screeched to a halt, as people lost their jobs, as everyone retreated into their homes, it was the doctors, nurses, first responders, police, firefighters, truck drivers, food suppliers, food workers, and teachers who became essential workers in those first few months of shutdown.

By the following September, it was often the nation's teachers who were called out for delays in returning to in-person instruction. But these decisions were not in the hands of classroom teachers! State governments set specific back-to-school protocols that schools had to follow. Those protocols included tweaking curriculum, redesigning instruction, rearranging furniture to meet six-foot distance markers, and turning school gymnasiums into school cafeterias by setting up hundreds of chairs six feet apart every day and taking them down every day. They also mandated that we amass safety supplies, such as COVID-19 tests, hand-sanitizing wipes, room-cleaning sprays, plexiglass desk shields, and masks, and that we follow contact-tracing protocols and establish in-school isolation rooms for symptomatic staff and students and staff vaccinations.

Teachers: We bore the brunt of parent complaints about the protocols that had to be followed. At board meetings, parents would publicly ask, "Why are the teachers wearing masks? Why is the teacher sitting behind a shield? My child can't have a teacher who is wearing a mask and face shield! It is the teacher's room; she can do what she wants in there." The last one is a statement furthest from the truth.

Teachers have been made out to be villains for the deficiencies and failures of our public school systems, exacerbated by the pandemic, but teachers have had enough. If teachers were overwhelmed before the COVID-19 pandemic, now we are mentally, emotionally, and physically exhausted and no longer willing to be blamed misguidedly.

COVID-19 was a turning point for teachers. We were frustrated that as a collective group we had little decision-making power, were doing our very best under extreme conditions, and yet were being criticized for simply following directives. What classroom teachers had always experienced was exacerbated by COVID-19. Many teachers retired, others left the profession outright, and news organizations reported on the difficulties teachers were facing.

In the fall of 2023, all school districts across America reported teacher shortages, and "interest in the teaching profession among high school seniors and college [freshmen] has fallen 50% since the 1990s and 38% since 2010, reaching the lowest level in the last fifty years. The number of new entrants into the profession has fallen by roughly one third over the last decade."[2]

If these trends continue, there will be no one facilitating the learning in the classroom.[3]

Therefore, it's critical that we teachers make sure to use our voices whenever we can.

Shake Off Some Responsibility

Over winter break, I met a teacher-colleague at the local veterinarian's office. As we chatted, our conversation turned to how difficult education, the profession, had become.

Of course, being a classroom teacher has always involved getting up at the crack of dawn, instructing up to 150 students a day, every day, for 8 hours, for 187 days. Teachers have always had to write engaging lessons, then teach the material and assess that their students have mastered the content and skills. Teachers have always taken work home at night and added 2 or more hours to their actual workday. Weekends for teachers have always involved hours spent planning for the following week. Combine those responsibilities with grading nightly papers, writing student recommendations, running lunch and after-school clubs, and managing those 25–150 students so that all learners can learn in engaging, respectful, and safe learning environments. Our common lament is that we do not have enough hours in a day to finish all our professional responsibilities, let alone those related to family and home. How, then, do teachers prioritize making their work responsibilities manageable?

The Evolving Responsibilities of Classroom Teachers

Since the inception of organized educational systems in this country, the primary responsibility of the classroom teacher was instructing—"teaching"—academic learning standards. When the COVID-19 pandemic hit, "teaching" academic concepts and skills and holding students responsible for "learning" them were no longer important. Teachers did the best we could, instructing from our homes, knowing our students were without necessary supplies, often watching lessons from their beds and not responsible for content mastery.

In that moment of history, the role of teacher took on a new responsibility—to keep a watchful eye, through a computer camera, on the "health" of our students. Teachers were now tasked with watching for signs of emotional, mental, and social distress and to immediately report to school support staff members. We needed to keep track of which students showed up for virtual class, which had their cameras on, which were dressed and out of bed. Conversely, we had to keep lists of students who were absent for Zoom class, who were logged in but had their cameras turned off, who had their cameras turned toward the ceiling, and who looked as if they might be in crisis.

To be clear, teachers have always been on the front lines of identifying children in distress—the child who woke up late one morning and didn't have time to eat breakfast, the child who had a fight with their best friend while on the school bus, the child who has a younger sibling with severe needs, or even the child who is in an abusive situation in the home. Teachers know their students so well that we can spot an issue immediately. But COVID-19 created emotional, social, and mental distress in practically *every* student, and they bring these distresses into classrooms where the frontline teachers bear the brunt of triaging student situations and issues. Teachers are now viewed as first responders when a student presents with a mental, emotional, or social health issue in the classroom.[4]

To address these new teacher responsibilities, a well-spring of social-emotional learning programs is now part of many school curricula. School support teams work within classrooms alongside teachers to develop self-awareness, self-control, and interpersonal skills that are necessary for school, future work, and life success. COVID-19 revealed *and* intensified that young people had little in the way of coping skills for everyday challenges. As a result, teachers have the added responsibility of building student character through developing better emotional, mental, and social health instructional mechanisms in our classrooms.

Never before have teachers felt such a responsibility within the education system to address students' mental health. Teacher expertise once limited to content instruction and assessment must now have an emphasis on developing personal and interpersonal skills within the classroom setting.

Using Your Voice Inside the Classroom

Managing work responsibilities, by using your voice, is the key to keeping priorities straight as additional responsibilities are layered upon us by school administration.

In order for teachers to prioritize their work responsibilities, we must first realize our primary responsibility as a classroom teacher is instructing—teaching—academic learning standards. When pulled away from these tasks, start using the phrases "my time is valuable" and "no, I cannot take that on at this moment."

Knowing your union contract is a *must* for all teachers. Consider your prep periods sacred. Be aware of the types of professional development you are being asked to attend, and make sure it is relevant to your pedagogical goals. If it is not, speak to colleagues, and then as a unified group, speak with your district curriculum team to voice your concerns.

Ask school leadership for a district organizational chart detailing who is responsible for what. Always check the chart so you know who is in charge, because outside of your classroom, you are not that person. Advocate that added responsibilities should be compensated with time or money.

Remember, voices are generally heard faster and taken more seriously the greater the number of voices.

Using Your Voice Outside the Classroom

Teachers use their voices to advocate on behalf of our students. Teachers use their voices to speak up and to speak out about the inequities that exist within school systems. Teachers use their voices in support of their colleagues. Teachers use their voices to support or oppose state and federal education laws. Teachers use their voices in everything we do while doing our jobs.

To use your voice outside of your classroom effectively, get active. Become a district mentor to new teachers, join district committees, or become a PTA district liaison. Run for a position in your district teacher's union or in your state teacher's union. Write opinion pieces for education periodicals, and keep informed on local, state, and federal educational issues.

In a groundbreaking research study, Pew Research directly asked thousands of K–12 teachers: "If there's one thing you'd want the public to know about teachers, what would it be?" Respondents cited common answers like "teaching is hard," "we care deeply about our student successes," "we need support from our parents," and "we need support from our administration." But the most telling response from a teacher's perspective was "we are undervalued and disrespected." Digging deeper, the research showed "Americans are about evenly divided on whether the public's perspective generally looks up to (32%) or down on (30%) public K–12 teachers. Some 37% say Americans neither look up to or down on public K–12 teachers."[5] The all-important work of America's teachers on the development of young people to lead our country into the future has a whopping 67 percent negative or neutral opinion of the work we do. Teacher-colleagues: Heed this research-based call to action, to stand together and voice the importance of the work we do.

Albert Einstein even knew the incredible power of a voice when he stated, "Be a voice, not an echo." In my home office, I have a very large, framed print of Einstein's quote, which is what my students saw during our Zoom classes.

Voice is a powerful vehicle to express your unique perspective, expertise, and ideas. It is never too early to teach the power of voice, and it is never too early to use your voice to effect positive change.

KEY TAKEAWAYS

Use your voice to effect change.

- "Finding your voice" is the ability to express your opinions, ideas, truths, and expertise with passion and power.
- To blame teachers for the failings within our public education system is misguided at best and self-defeating at worst, as we have little to no power within the system.
- Teachers report to many stakeholders—state education departments, school board members, district leadership, school leadership, department heads, colleagues, team teachers, parents, and students.
- Use your voice to advocate on behalf of others.
- Use your voice to advocate on behalf of yourself.
- Use your voice to convey content and to encourage, motivate, praise, and celebrate student successes.
- Use your voice to speak up about inequities within the school system.

- Use your voice to support or oppose local, state, and federal education policies and laws.
- Advocate that certain added responsibilities should be compensated with time or money.

Part 3

A TEACHER'S GUIDE TO SELF-CARE

Each morning, more than one teacher enters our school building with rolling carts and carry-on luggage pieces tightly packed with binders, folders overflowing with student work, textbooks, and student workbooks. I am in the annoying habit of saying to my colleagues, "Hurry up, Flight 32 is boarding at Gate 12. If you don't run, you will miss your flight." My sass doesn't go over very well, but it is very effective in pointing out the absurdity of these very dedicated teachers taking so much work and materials home after an already ten-hour workday that they need a suitcase to carry it all.

Teachers: We are very good at taking care of others but fail miserably at tending to our own needs, especially now when stressors, disruptions, and crises are normal parts of our everyday work life. How do we cultivate a mindset of gratitude? How do we surround ourselves with colleagues who will lift us up when knocked down, brush us off, and stand by our side? How do we prioritize ourselves so we can be our best in and out of our classrooms? How do we reduce our work-related responsibilities to gain a needed and better work-life balance? How do we find the confidence to map out next steps when the ones we have been walking no longer feel right or fulfilling?

Come, teachers, it's time to focus on ourselves, using a teacher's guide to self-care.

LESSON 10

Be Grateful

December 2024 finds me finishing this book's revised manuscript exactly five years to the initial COVID-19 news coming out of Wuhan, China. The palpable fear of that once-emerging virus has faded, but living through a once-in-a-hundred-years pandemic that had 6,805,271 cases reported in the state of New York, with 1 in 243 residents having died from the coronavirus, a total of over 84,000 deaths, left permanent effects.[1]

Even as the virus has since retreated, other disruptors have crept into the classroom lives of students and teachers. Though these distractors are serious, we teachers continue to focus on the good, the positive, and the empowering to give gratitude center stage.

There Are Always Positives— Just Look for Them

My mother's oldest sister died at the height of COVID-19 while living in a nursing facility, preventing a traditional funeral and family final goodbyes. My son suffered disappointments including leaving friends and his college internship, missing his college graduation, and then enduring half his graduate degree earned in front of a computer screen in his childhood bedroom. My daughter struggled to keep her own elementary school children on task while remote teaching from her kitchen table.

Yet during the last five years, my son did earn his master's in public policy and has his dream policy position in Connecticut's capital. On schedule, my daughter received her tenure and is a very much-loved and respected elementary school educator in her school district. During lockdown, her girlfriend made the decision to go after her lifelong dream and is now enrolled in college and halfway through working toward her BS in veterinary technology and licensure. Even in the darkest times, there are periods of light that must be acknowledged and celebrated.

Counting My Blessings

On a personal level, I was grateful each day. I was grateful for my health, my children's health, my elderly parents' health, my siblings' health, and my coworkers' health. I was grateful to still be working and earning a paycheck with quality health insurance. I was grateful my children were still working or in school engaging their minds in productive ways. I was grateful to still have personal connections to colleagues and students. I was grateful to still be useful and have purpose, which kept my mind productively occupied rather than needlessly worried.

Some coworkers retired during the COVID-19 lockdown or the following academic year. National statistics reported 567,000 fewer educators in public schools than there were before the pandemic.[2]

For those of us who stayed, we were pushed to our limits. I cannot even count in the first two years of the pandemic how many times teachers were exposed to COVID-19, how many times we searched for COVID-19 testing sites, or how often we suffered through COVID-19 symptoms. I know all teachers will agree that we tried our professional best to be an academic and social/emotional guidepost for our students.

Teachers: Take a Bow

Even through those trying days, teachers recognized, as did the country, that we had the ability to help during this devastating health crisis. Throughout the pandemic, teachers were considered among the non–health-care essential worker heroes. We showed up in face shields and face masks, ate alone, and kept six feet from everyone, but we showed up every single day to provide a sense of normalcy through instruction.

Teachers were thanked, lauded, and applauded. The genuine outpouring of teacher appreciation helped get us through those early months, and we were grateful to be recognized for the work and support we provided.

Gratitude: A Necessary Mindset

Gratitude is powerful. Research shows being grateful has positive social, emotional, and psychological benefits, as it focuses on the good during bad times. Harvard Health reports that gratitude helps people feel more positive emotions, relish good experiences, improve their health, deal with adversity, and build strong relationships.[3] These benefits enhance our self-care by making our physical, emotional, and mental health more resilient. Even in our darkest moments, we must be cognizant of life's blessings and be grateful. Focusing on the positives is a necessary mindset—not only during crises, but every day.

KEY TAKEAWAYS

Gratitude is necessary for a positive mindset.

- In every situation, look hard for the positives.
- Accept recognition and appreciation for doing your best.
- Gratitude is a powerful change agent.
- Gratitude should be a mindful tool in your self-care practices.

LESSON 11

Find Your Work Family

Schools are weird places to work at for adults. In my school, all teaching staff are generally in the building no later than 7:00 a.m. for a start time of 7:30 a.m. We spend the bulk of our days surrounded by and interacting primarily with children or young adults. For myself, that would be young people ages twelve through sixteen. Teachers are in their classrooms for seven hours a day, and after-school office hours and professional meetings usually extend our workdays another hour or two. The only times we are in the company of other adults is if we have a co-teacher in the class or if we have a common lunch or prep period where teachers sit in the same space.

By the nature of our duties, the workday can be isolating for a teacher. Much of our adult conversations are limited to a minute or two during a change of period or an unexpected meetup in hallways. During actual meeting time, all discussion is focused on student issues, parent meetings, or administrative tasks. Yes, we often find a bit of time to listen to a colleague walk through a student or parent concern and how they handled it or for input on an instructional issue while walking to a meeting, running to the restroom, or heading out at the end of the day. But for the most part, teachers are alone in our classes with our students, devoid of other adult contact.

Experienced teachers are used to and adept at changing and wearing our many hats in adult isolation. Brand-new teachers, however, often find the first year or two or five to be overwhelming. Though teaching is a job done without the luxury of adult collaboration, adult support is very much needed, and that became very clear to us teachers while not just teaching through a pandemic, but also any crisis.

A New Kind of Isolation

Thrown into the chaos of online instruction; fears for our own physical health and that of our family members; watching our world shrink overnight; and feeling the emotional, social, and mental impact that had on our own children and ourselves, turning to our professional colleagues helped get teachers through those early pandemic months, March 2020 to the end of that school year in June 2020.

Our school support team hand delivered boxes of Edible Arrangements to every teacher. My own teaching team scheduled Zoom happy hours on Friday afternoons. Not one teacher complained at the scheduled Zoom faculty meetings, because it was reassuring to see each other, albeit on a screen. Faculty directories were distributed with our cell phone numbers for easy texting, and more often than not, texting began in the predawn hours and ended often past midnight. Those moments spent in Zoom faculty meetings allowed us to focus on something tangible—our work—and forget the unknowns of the pandemic swirling around us. Texting colleagues about student issues allowed us to step outside of our personal worries and concentrate on others. Posting laugh emojis to a colleague's reel postings allowed us to feel—even for a minute—that pre-pandemic silliness. Human connection during a time of forced isolation was critical for our professional success as well as our personal well-being.

Among the many lessons we can take away from surviving through the pandemic, or any type of small or large crisis, is the importance of human connection, even more so in isolating professions like teaching. Isolation forced us to see the importance of social connections and that as humans we are social beings.

Teacher besties are a must-have for our own mental and emotional health and general well-being. All professionals live their own "daily work grind," and it is critical to have besties who experience a daily grind similar to your own. Our besties "get that," "live it," "understand it," "thrive at it," and as such are invaluable supports for our professional success and personal health. Besties provide a listening ear, a caring shoulder, on-point collaboration, a classroom break, and an extra dose of authentic positive feedback.[1]

The Best of Besties

As teachers, our work family understands the joys of the work we do and the stressors that easily drain us. Our work family shares our values and goals as educators and provides support and encouragement for our aspirations and dreams. Our work family is eager to help us, listen to us, teach us, calm us, and propel us to bigger and better. Our work family thinks we can do anything. Our work family simply gets us, and many surveyed teachers agree:

- Brittany R., a first-grade classroom teacher, describes her work besties as "my family. My support system in and out of the school building. These are my trusted core four who I go to vent to after rough moments and providers of comic relief when needed. My work besties share the same passion for the work I do."

- Erika C., a middle school content teacher, believes "work besties are critical. They are there for us in our silly moments and climb into the trench with us to support us when we are at our lowest. They laugh with us, remind us of our strengths, and listen-listen-listen."
- Cheila M., a high school honors content teacher, describes hers as "loyal, smart, and funny!!! They make me smile every day."
- Kaylan R., an elementary reading specialist, describes her work besties as "literally everything. They are what gets me through the day. They are the only people in my life who get what I'm going through daily. They are my inspiration and my motivation; they keep my sanity in check."
- Sandy A., a middle school content teacher, reminds us that "camaraderie isn't always a given in the workplace so when you are lucky enough to have amazing work colleagues who are supportive, they can make the most challenging work environments enjoyable."
- Lori W. faces challenges "head-on and [has] learned to lean on colleagues for guidance and support."

Building Your Work Family

So how do teachers cultivate an in-school support system? To build your work family, first get to know your teaching colleagues. Your grade-level teaching colleagues for elementary teachers or your team-level colleagues and department colleagues for middle and high school teachers are the colleagues you work with and interact with the most on any given day. But just as we should be advising our students, we need to step out of our comfort zones, too. During faculty meetings, professional development workshops, and lunch in the teachers' lounge, sit with teachers you may not know very well. Getting to know all the teaching staff, or at least more of the teaching staff, will widen your bestie circle.

Once you make initial connections, be proactive and purposefully seek out colleagues who will make you laugh, have your back no matter what, and think you are amazing as a person as well as at your profession. Deepen connections with colleagues who you have discovered share similar dreams and aspirations.

If you and a colleague see the need to start a school literary magazine, work together to get one up and running. If you and your colleague are thinking about working toward a reading license, see if there are any online classes you can take together. Once you have found your family, start a group chat, eat lunch together, spend prep periods together, or grab a quick bite to eat together before catching the school musical or after the last varsity football game of the season. Celebrating important personal occasions in and out of the school building deepens bonds in unexpected ways as well.

Teachers spend much of their professional lives in the company of young people, so we must find our adult work family. In-school support systems are critically important for a teacher's social, emotional, and mental health. Your work family will celebrate your successes and help see you through crises as minor as not making enough worksheet copies and as major as teaching in isolation. Build your work family to fulfill the human need of *belonging* while motivating yourself to be the best teacher you can be while in your classroom.

KEY TAKEAWAYS

Building a work family is essential to your social, emotional, and mental health and professional success.

- Seek out colleagues who share your basic personal and professional values, goals, dreams, and aspirations.
- Seek out colleagues who readily provide work-related support, such as running a few copies, covering your class in a pinch, or even doing a quick coffee run.

- Seek out colleagues who will have your back—no matter what.
- When you find one, two, three, or even four colleagues who fit the bill, nurture those relationships.

LESSON 12

Put Yourself First

Teaching is stressful work, and being a teacher can be mentally, physically, and emotionally exhausting. True teachers willingly make the decision to be in the classroom, but that does not take away from the realities of navigating the day-to-day responsibilities, which are often changing and challenging. State-driven emergency drills, including fire, lockdown, lockout, and shelter in place, are necessary but cut into precious instructional time and unnerve our already anxious students.

Coming out of COVID-19, many have a clearer awareness of the necessity of taking care of their own health, with district policies supporting staff taking sick days for self and family members, which often leads to in-school staff covering classes and losing our precious in-school planning time.

Another effect of the teacher shortage is the universal substitute teacher shortage. Normally, if a colleague is absent, a teacher is asked to fill in during their own professional or preparation period. On a "normal" school day, turning state-driven, content-learning standards into curriculum lessons, instructing between 25 and 150 students every day, grading between 25 and 150 multi-assessments each night, and prepping for the next day's work leaves teachers feeling tired and often burnt out from their average twelve-to-fourteen-hour days. When teachers have days off throughout the school year, we often catch up on sleep, appointments, and family responsibilities. For most teachers, "overwhelmed" is a natural state of being, which is why it is critical to find the time to practice self-care each day.

Teaching Calm When Classroom Life Is Stressful

School communities face many types of crises where district policies and procedures get little input from classroom teachers, including the most serious situations—pandemics, school shootings, bullying, and teen suicides. As educators, we have to create ways to keep ourselves calm. But how do you keep calm when your classroom can feel stressful or under siege?

When this question was posed to educators, most agreed that *calm* is not a word generally used to describe many situations that involve young people ages five through seventeen in classroom settings. Survey respondent Janis B. not surprisingly asked, "Calm? What is calm?"

Over 15 percent of teacher respondents unequivocally agreed that "faith and daily meditation are anchors for successful school days." Mary D., a retired inner-city teacher, shared, "I used to pray daily for my students and their families. When a crisis arose, I was able to pray for guidance in the situation and act with confidence and peace." Sonia A., a current elementary special education classroom teacher, relies on "starting the day with quiet meditation." Aubrey P., a middle school English language arts teacher, concurs and "completes meditations even before having my first cup of morning coffee." Laura S. relies on "chocolate and caffeine." Arline D. suggests "taking classes or downloading apps in yoga, wall Pilates, and breathing exercises."

When it comes to the myriads of smaller, always inconvenient, and frustrating crises teachers are confronted with daily—like the copy machines being down for a week, your school computer crashing, or three new students being added to your class roster and you having no physical room for them—keeping calm for yourself and your students is vital to the flow, structure, and tone of your every-day, every-period classroom environment. Faith, calming meditation, and some kind of physical activity release—like ten minutes of wall or chair Pilates or even a quick walk around the school block during your lunch period—certainly have their place among stress-relieving strategies. And never underestimate the calming effect a small piece of chocolate can have after a long, stressful day.

Practice Self-Care Every Day

Self-care is the purposeful practice of taking care of your physical, mental, emotional, and social health so you can thrive as an individual. Self-care does not require large amounts of time or expensive equipment, only small doses of treasured or healthy activities that will reduce stress, recenter yourself, and improve your overall well-being.

There are many self-care resources available online, but what is most important is to understand that self-care is unique for everyone. Everyone has different self-care needs, so the first step is to evaluate your care goals and then plan to achieve them. In setting your goals, be mindful of what aspects of your health you want to focus on—physical, mental, emotional, or social.

No matter what your individualized plan develops into, all teachers should internalize these basic self-care steps:

- **Set and maintain firm contact boundaries.** Generally, an elementary school day is between the hours of 8:15 a.m. and 3:15 p.m., while middle and high schools are in session between 7:15 a.m.

and 3:30 p.m. These are your working hours, so stick to them.

- » Set a specific start and end time to your workday. Do not open work emails until you are at your classroom desk. Do not open work emails after a specific time each afternoon. Let me add a caveat here: I do check my emails in the evening, but I only open and respond to those from students or parents reaching out with a true emergency that needs an immediate response. This situation must be the exception, not the rule.
- » Decide with your teaching team what these times will be, so you are consistent with work practices.
- » During weekends and vacation days, set a "Not in Classroom" message with specifics of when you can be expected to return emails.
- » Limit teaching team texts on weeknights and weekends.
- » In parent correspondence, sign off with your full name with the expectation that parents will address you as the professional you are and not by your first name.

- **Ditch the rolling luggage.** Invest in a professional carryall, and leave the rolling luggage, carts, and wagons at home. If your nightly work to be graded cannot fit in a large professional bag, then you are taking too much work home.

- **Understand you have little control.** Data reveals that teachers make 4 decisions every minute of their workday, 1,500 decisions every school day, for a total of 280,500 decisions every school year.[1]
- **This decision fatigue is yet another reason for self-care.** But the majority of these decisions arise from situations that are out of the classroom teacher's control, which leads to our increased worry, anxiety, and stress. Be mindful of what is in your control as a classroom teacher and what is not. Follow these strategies to cut down on decision fatigue and what it brings:
  - » Make your morning routine less stressful by packing up the night before, laying out your outfit for the day, and having a nutritious but simple breakfast.
  - » On your way to school, listen to an audiobook, favorite sports radio, or music, or bask in the silence and beauty of the early morning drive.
  - » Aim to arrive at your school with at least fifteen minutes of quiet time. I enter my room but only turn on one bright classroom light to ease into my morning. I keep my door locked

to dissuade well-meaning colleagues from stopping by. Fifteen minutes of solitude helps ready you for what is usually a hectic day.

  - » Softly playing classical music in the background while students are working naturally brings some order back to the class.
  - » If your teaching period and students have taken a turn toward chaos, stop the lesson and gather students for a five-minute breathing or seated yoga exercise or two. Calming brings back some control when feeling out of control.
  - » At lunchtime or even during a prep period, step outside into the fresh air. Walk around the block, stand in front of the school building with the sun on your face, or mindfully listen to nature.
  - » Keep a reading book handy for some escapism. On particularly stressful days, I go to our school library and find a Nancy Drew novel—nothing like bringing my cortisol levels down by reading a favorite childhood book.

- **Keep your successes visible.** Teachers often lose sight of the positive impacts we have made with the thousands of students we have taught. Our successes fill us with joy and motivation, so keep them front and center.

- » Keep positive notes and thank-you cards from students and parents on display and reread them often. Many teachers have bulletin boards for such displays in classrooms and home offices.
- » When a student has a shining moment, send a quick, personalized email to the student, parents, guidance staff, and administration. Student success is a reflection of teacher success. Everyone should celebrate!
- » Write personalized "caught you being great" notes in the moment.
- » For every parent phone call made for a negative reason, make a second parent phone call for a positive reason. The parent on the other end of the phone will be shocked and thrilled to hear from you, which will keep you beaming for at least an hour.
- » Send copies of positive emails from parents to your administrators.
- » As students are working, take photos to send to admin with a short write-up.

In addition to those basic practices, self-care should be individualized, practiced purposefully every day, and in small doses across all health areas. Following this action plan will help create the habit of consistency, which will lead to permanent healthy changes. To get you started, here are strategies organized as simple or ongoing for those activities that bring you contentment.

SIMPLE

- Never underestimate silence and solitude so you can listen to yourself.
- Take in nature with a lunchtime or free period walk around the block.
- Play background sounds—rainfall, waterfall, ocean waves, wind, or birds.
- Play music.
- Get moving by parking at the end of the school parking lot to get those extra steps in.
- Keep a free weight or kettlebell in your classroom for some weight work.
- Keep books or printouts on easy-to-do wall or chair yoga.
- Take a decompression walk after school before you go home.
- Switch out one unhealthy food for a healthier one.
- Meditate, stretch, or dance.

- Practice mindfulness.
- Listen to your self-talk.

ONGOING

- Start a new hobby or restart an old one.
- Get involved with a volunteer organization.
- Connect with friends and family on a school night.
- Journal your thoughts, feelings, experiences, and dreams. This is how I started writing this book!
- Find a professional therapist if the stress of the job is too much for you to handle on your own.

Teachers are in the business of taking care of others; it is what we do and who we are. Teachers are so conditioned to put everyone else's needs before our own that self-care can seem indulgent. Teachers must purposefully practice taking care of our physical, mental, emotional, and social health every day so we can thrive as individuals. Small doses of treasured or healthy activities will reduce stress, recenter ourselves, and improve our overall well-being.

KEY TAKEAWAYS

Putting yourself first is necessary for your best self.

- Stick to your contractual working hours.
- Take a small amount of work home, if at all.
- Practice strategies that will keep you calm in your often chaotic classroom.
- Keep your successes front and center.
- Individualize your self-care and practice daily.

LESSON 13

Chart Your Own Course and Always Look Ahead

Teaching through a pandemic is difficult—really, really, *really* difficult. Up until the start of COVID-19, I had taught for thirty years in both inner-city and suburban districts. I had taught children below grade level, on grade level, and surpassing grade-level competencies. I taught students who could not wait to enter my classroom to learn new content and those who dreaded even walking into the school building. I taught students who had endured trauma and rose above it and those who were buried under its weight. I am considered a master teacher—a teacher with more than one teaching certificate who can turn any classroom with any type of student into a caring, student-centered, successful learning environment.

Yet teaching through a pandemic was so hard that, upon returning to school in the fall of 2020, I gave serious thought to retirement for the following June, believing I had nothing left to give to my students. Retirement was such a real possibility for me that when I returned to the classroom in the fall of 2020, I slowly but deliberately started emptying my file cabinets and transporting all my instructional materials to my home office. Then the 2021–22 school year "return to normalcy" was the most challenging year of my entire academic professional career.

Developing a Five-Year Plan

The pandemic gave me the time and reason to rethink my life's journey up until that moment and follow my dad's advice to "always look ahead." For the first time, I had this overwhelming need to take control of my professional life.

Working for a school district is constraining at best and stifling at worst. At the same time, teaching through COVID-19 forced me to take stock of my current professional life and begin to think about my future professional plans in terms of developing a five-year plan. Having worked in education for thirty years, I realized that retirement was inching closer and could be my reality by the end of that five-year plan. On this road to "looking ahead," I knew I needed to take the time to look back and reflect on what I had already achieved professionally, what I was still interested in doing, and what I should let go of.

I was sure of a few things. First, I knew I wanted to start a small educational consulting business. I carved out three years to move it from the research stage to the up-and-running stage. Second, I knew I needed to develop, design, and run my business's website. Last, I knew I wanted to document my experiences teaching through COVID-19. Initially, I didn't know if I had a book in me, but I did carve out three years for this project as well. I wrote for one year, sent out my rough manuscript cold to literary agents and then to publishers, and after six months, started discussions with Greenleaf, the publisher behind this book.

Three Keys to Discover Your Future Self

As I reflected on my path forward in 2020, I considered the three big "life at a crossroads" questions: What was I good at, what did I still like to do, and what needs would my interests and talents fill? In reflecting, I seriously thought about whether I wanted to stay in the classroom for the next decade—probably not—though I had always had a talent for teaching, writing curriculum, and training new teachers. Even if I walked out and away from a physical classroom, I knew for certain that I still wanted to be involved in the work of educating students and training teachers on how to accomplish that vital work.

Many retired colleagues had taken part-time jobs as adjuncts at local colleges, and some had even become teacher trainers at area school districts. I knew I had no desire to work for another district or in a classroom setting as a teacher since I had "been there and done that." The decision of what direction to take postretirement would take more time, serious thought, and endless research.

The idea that kept bouncing around my mind was centered on my experience teaching through a pandemic. As an experienced, confident, and successful educator, I was amazed at the level of support I required during those initial months of teaching through the pandemic—much like the support I needed throughout my very first year of teaching. At the time, I chided myself for needing that support. After all, I had been in this business of education for thirty years, but the amount of time didn't matter. What mattered was that when faced with any tremendous change, new teachers and experienced teachers need more support, not less, than in their day-to-day, and in that moment, an idea simply crystallized.

I would transform my years of experience and expertise into a new format: a web-based educational consulting start-up, InOurClassrooms, LLC, where I could help other educators navigate this difficult but rewarding profession called teaching.

In addition to a newfound passion for starting my

own consulting business, during the early days of the pandemic, I had started handwriting a journal of my teaching experiences. Two years later, I was still writing consistently, though I admittedly did switch to digital journaling. I knew, both as a trained public health official and as an educator, that we were living through a historical event, one I wanted to document my experiences with. I periodically would read through my journal entries. As I reread those typed notes, I realized I had the beginnings of a manuscript, which I immediately titled *Life Lessons Learned While Teaching Through a Pandemic: Insights of a Veteran Educator*.

Following my dad's advice, looking ahead for me meant starting to plan my next five years. Looking ahead meant wanting my voice and my experiences heard. Looking ahead meant wanting to start a consulting business, writing a book on my pandemic experiences, helping young teachers and anyone figuring out the important lessons to live their professional lives by. Looking ahead made me see myself somewhere other than in a classroom, and my brain was swirling with so many ideas that I often focused on little else.

Becoming Your Future Self

At night, in the early morning hours, and on weekend afternoons, I started editing, adding to, and refining my original journal entries, and before I knew it, hours had passed. My schoolwork took a back seat to this new project, but I felt a rush of creativity and excitement I had not felt in decades. Slowly but surely, a nonfiction book was taking shape.

Once the world reopened, I checked my local Barnes & Noble and Amazon booksellers to see if any other teacher had written a book like mine—any author needs to keep up with their competition. I friended many of my favorite authors on Facebook just to see a glimpse of what their writing lives were like. I attended any local author event to hear their publishing experiences and any encouraging words they could offer. When my rough manuscript was completed, I started sending it out cold to agents. I held tightly to any small encouraging words—"There is a lot to like about your process" and "Do not stop until you find the right agent or publisher"—that came in the many rejection letters.

The only person I confided my book project to was my college bestie, a *New York Times* bestseller herself, Charmaine Wilkerson, author of *Black Cake* and *Good Dirt*. When she heard I had a manuscript, she said, "Annie, you were always such a good writer, just don't give up!" Next, I let my children in on my "secret project," about which they could not be more supportive.

When I wasn't working on my developing manuscript, I was focusing on starting a small educational consultant business for when I did submit my retirement papers. I kept this to myself as well because I wanted to present a finished idea to my children to show the seriousness of my future business plan. I spent months purchasing books on how to create a brand; how to use Instagram, Facebook, and X (formerly Twitter) to your best advantage; how to start an LLC; and how to create a website. My bookshelves are overflowing with "how to" texts. I took inspiration from my home office as I decided on the name, created a logo, and began the process of the business becoming an LLC. My teal, gray, and black home office was purposely designed to be calming, empowering, and motivational. I have a large print of Einstein's quote "Be a voice, not an echo" next to a large wall-mounted directional compass. I have inspirational quotes scattered throughout to remind me to be defined by who I am, what I want to achieve, and what my strengths are.

My small business is now an LLC with clients, and my website is up and steadily gaining notice through my growing audience on social media. When I do formally retire—no date in mind—I will have my business to keep me busy and creatively engaged. Oh, and that manuscript born of short journal entries that I envisioned being published? Well, you are reading it!

You in Five Years

When my father was in his midnineties, he and my mom, in her early nineties, were seriously discussing redoing their kitchen. My father expected to continue to live a long, healthy life alongside my mom, and they wanted a new kitchen to enjoy for the coming years. The pandemic delayed their kitchen redo, and my dad passed in the spring of 2021, but his message was his legacy. Thinking about and acting on what you want to achieve in the future is the way to live. No matter what is happening in your present day, always look ahead.

For me, a pandemic spurred me to reevaluate my life and set it in a focused direction, but how do you know what direction to take when you are ready for a professional change? Looking ahead definitely needs the right attitude, the belief that it is important, and the knowledge that the present is temporary. But a structured plan is also necessary for your new course of action.

First, you must determine what is in your current life—that which you love and that which you are ready to change—and what is propelling you into your future self. What do you want your future self and life to look like? What are the most important facets of your future life? Take a significant amount of time to reflect on areas of professional and personal expertise. In this same light, analyze both your professional and personal strengths and weaknesses. Next is for you to identify your professional skill sets and your personal skill sets. Brainstorming ideas that reflect your expertise, skill sets, and creativity is necessary before you begin the task of researching each possible idea.

Once you see what you want to do, then you can go

about planning concrete steps that will secure your future self. Realize what you can control in that moment. You will need to create an action plan with a timetable and then methodically tick off each action item as you complete it. Professional change begins with one concrete idea that you should listen to. Strategize an action plan to transform the idea into your future.

KEY TAKEAWAYS

The way to move forward is through looking ahead. Focus on what you envision for your future and start working toward it.

- Believe in the importance of looking ahead.
- Look ahead to the "future" you.
- What is most important to the future you?
- Make concrete lists of what steps need to be taken to realize that future you.
- Complete the steps you can do now that will secure your future you.
- Reflect on areas of professional and personal expertise.
- Identify your professional skill sets.
- Identify your personal skill sets.

- Brainstorm ideas that reflect your expertise, skill sets, and creativity.
- Create an action plan and timeline.
- Methodically tick off each action item as you complete it.

Some Final Thoughts

DECEMBER 9, 2024

Initially, writing these "final thoughts" was the most difficult of my 32,000-plus written words. My editors suggested I reread the entire manuscript and share my thoughts on "where we started (the brink of a pandemic) and where we are now (never-ending stressors and classroom crises)." I did not want to reword, restate, or rehash my previous points. I certainly wanted to leave you, my teacher-colleagues, with some wise, uplifting words, but I was at a complete loss as to what those words would be. And then I received a LinkedIn message that crystallized exactly what my final thoughts to you would be.

The message, sent last week, read:

Dear Ms. Richter,

I am so glad I found you on LinkedIn. My brother and I went to JHS 113, 1989–1992. Ms. Shanda was my brother's math teacher and instrumental in his education and future. He has been trying to get in touch with her for a while. Any information you may have on her would be greatly appreciated. My brother Tim and I are originally from India. We were fresh off the boat back then, and as they say, it takes a village . . . We are grateful for teachers like you!

Katrina Lovely

The pandemic passed, and we survived. New and different crises roll through our classrooms, and we survive. I wrote this book to put the focus on us to be our very best, so our students can be their very best and move forward into successful lives.

In my introduction, I wrote, "Most importantly, I hope this book reignites your passion and purpose as a classroom teacher." Tim Lovely, thirty-five years later, is trying to find his middle school math teacher to say thank you and "you were instrumental in my education and in my life."

Every teacher has at least one Tim Lovely. There is no other profession that has such a profound impact on others like teaching does. Teacher-colleagues, never lose sight that we do incredibly important work in our classrooms.

Acknowledgments

I am incredibly indebted to my Greenleaf Team. Steve Elizalde, thank you for not being scared off by my over-the-top enthusiasm. Lee Reed Zarnikau, thank you for believing in my abilities as a writer and for embracing this project with such positivity, as an editor and as a parent. Tess Newton, thank you for your clarity and insight and always making my words flow and read so much better. Lee and Tess, together, thank you for helping me realize my dream of being a published author.

I am the teacher I am today thanks to the teacher besties, school staff, and former administrators at MS 113, Bronx, New York: Mark Dineen, Stacey Schultz, Fred Polvere, Alan Patton, Harold Hoffman, Helen Degnan, Venessa Singleton, Bonnie Esposito, Vivi McGuire, Frank Uzzo, Tom DeGrazia, and Julia Swann. A loving look upward to my angel besties Esther Ravin, Noreen Fuerstman, Carol Reid, and our beloved Danny Marblo.

Fast-forward twenty-five-plus years, and I could not have been in a better school district with better support as we weathered the pandemic together and continue to successfully move through every crisis together. To past and present administrators, guidance counselors, school support staff, and teachers of the middle and high school staff of the TUFSD: Besides my enthusiastic students and their supportive parents, you are the reason I want to come to work every day. A special shout-out to my irreplaceable besties: Meighan Collins-Carter, Erika Conway, Danielle Dwyer, Cheila Mosa, Patrick O'Connell, and Maureen Petrellesse.

To my children, Brittany and Jonathan, thank you for being my biggest cheerleaders. When I told you I wrote a manuscript, you were even more excited than I was! Thank you for supporting my dream of being an author. I love you both to the moon and back! I am incredibly proud that you are following your dreams. Jonathan, every day you are impacting the lives of Connecticut citizens by choosing a life of public service. Brittany, every day you are shaping the minds and lives of your first graders so they can grow up and achieve great things. Emily, as you and Brittany build your lives, you are making your dream of being a vet tech a reality. It is simply an honor and privilege to be your mom.

Resources

Teacher Resources

Bored Teachers: www.boredteachers.com

We Are Teachers: www.weareteachers.com

Teachers of Tomorrow: www.teachersoftomorrow.org

Teachers Pay Teachers: www.teacherspayteachers.com

Professional Journal for Teachers

Education Week: www.edweek.org

Professional Development Resources for Teachers

ASCD: ascd.org

Edutopia: www.edutopia.org

National Teacher Organizations

American Federation of Teachers: www.aft.org

National Education Association: www.nea.org

American Association of Colleges for Teacher Education: aacte.org

United States Department of Education Websites

US Department of Education: www.ed.gov

National Center for Education Statistics: nces.ed.gov

Your own state's Department of Education website

Notes

Introduction

1. Natalie P. McNeal, "As Fewer Students Seek Teaching Degrees, Universities Close Undergraduate Programs," TeacherCertification.com, 2025, https://teachercertification.com/fewer-students-seek-teaching-degrees/.

2. Alex Leeds Matthews, Amy O'Kruk, and Annette Choi, "School Shootings in the US: Fast Facts," CNN, last modified May 28,2025, https://www.cnn.com/us/school-shootings-fast-facts-dg/index.html.

3. US Centers for Disease Control and Prevention, *YRBS Data Summary & Trends Report: 2013–2023* (US Department of Health and Human Services, 2024), https://www.cdc.gov/yrbs/dstr/index.html.

4. National Center for Education Statistics, *Prevalence of Mental Health Services Provided by Public Schools and Limitations in Schools' Efforts to Provide Mental Health Services* (US Department of Education, 2024), https://nces.ed.gov/programs/coe/indicator/a23/school-mental-health-services?tid=4.

Lesson 4

1. Lindsey Pollak, "How to Toot Your Own Horn at Work—and Why That Matters," *iaee Blog Station*, February 17, 2022, https://www.iaee.com/2022/02/17/how-to-toot-your-own-horn-at-work-and-why-that-matters/.

Lesson 5

1. Amanda Musa, "US Confirmed Country's First Case of COVID-19 Three Years Ago Friday," CNN, January 20, 2023, https://www.cnn.com/2023/01/20/health/covid-three-years-us-case-confirmed/index.html; US Centers for Disease Control and Prevention, "CDC Museum COVID-19 Timeline," CDC, last reviewed July 8, 2024, https://www.cdc.gov/museum/timeline/covid19.html.
2. Christian Nolan, "Lawrence Garbuz, New York's First Known COVID-19 Case, Reveals What He Learned About Attorney Well-Being from the Virus," New York State Bar Association, August 11, 2020, https://nysba.org/lawrence-garbuz-new-yorks-first-known-covid-19-case-reveals-what-he-learned-about-attorney-well-being-from-the-virus/.
3. Allison Dunne, "Looking Back at COVID Beginning in New Rochelle," WAMC Northeast Public Radio, December 29, 2020, https://www.wamc.org/hudson-valley-news/2020-12-29/looking-back-at-covid-beginning-in-new-rochelle.
4. Mayo Clinic Staff, "Stress Relief from Laughter? It's No Joke," *Healthy Lifestyle* (blog), Mayo Clinic, September 22, 2023, https://www.mayoclinic.org/healthy-lifestyle/stress-management/in-depth/stress-relief/art-20044456.
5. Bored Teachers, "The Struggle Is Real" Comedy Tour, https://www.boredteachers.com/comedy-tour.

Lesson 6

1. Elizabeth A. Harris, "'It Was Just Too Much': How Remote Learning Is Breaking Parents," *The New York Times*, April 27, 2020, https://www.nytimes.com/2020/04/27/nyregion/coronavirus-homeschooling-parents.html.

Lesson 7

1. Sarah Mervosh, Claire Cain Miller, and Francesca Paris, "What the Data Says About Pandemic School Closures, Four Years Later," *The New York Times*, March 18, 2024, https://www.nytimes.com/2024/03/18/upshot/pandemic-school-closures-data.html.
2. Megan Kuhfeld, Jim Soland, Karyn Lewis, and Emily Morton, "The Pandemic Has Had Devastating Impacts on Learning. What Will It Take to Help Students Catch Up?" Brookings, March 3, 2022, https://www.brookings.edu/articles/the-pandemic-has-had-devastating-impacts-on-learning-what-will-it-take-to-help-students-catch-up/.
3. Laura Meckler and Lauren Lumpkin, "Four Years After COVID, Many Students Still Losing Ground," *The Washington Post*, July 23, 2024, https://www.washingtonpost.com/education/2024/07/23/covid-test-scores-learning-loss-absenteeism/.
4. Carol Dweck, *Mindset: The New Psychology of Success* (Random House, 2006).
5. Eleanor O'Rourke, Kyla Haimovitz, Christy Ballweber, Carol Dweck, and Zoran Popović, "Brain Points: A Growth Mindset Incentive Structure Boosts Persistence in an Educational Game," *CHI '14: Proceedings of the SIGCHI Conference on Human Factors in Computing Systems* (2014): 3339–48, https://doi.org/10.1145/2556288.2557157.

6. Betsy Ng, "The Neuroscience of Growth Mindset and Intrinsic Motivation," *Brain Sciences* 8, no. 2 (2018): 20, https://doi.org/10.3390/brainsci8020020.

Lesson 8

1. Jocelyn Gecker, "Kids Are Using Phones in Class, Even When It's Against the Rules. Should Schools Ban Them All Day?" *Education* (blog), Associated Press, last updated February 27, 2024, https://apnews.com/article/school-cell-phone-ban-01fd6293a84a2e4e401708b15cb71d36.
2. Anna Lamb, "Do Phones Belong in Schools?" *The Harvard Gazette*, March 13, 2023, https://news.harvard.edu/gazette/story/2023/03/experts-see-pros-and-cons-to-allowing-cellphones-in-class/.
3. The Learning Network, "What Students Are Saying About School Cellphone Bans," *The New York Times*, November 30, 2023, https://www.nytimes.com/2023/11/30/learning/what-students-are-saying-about-school-cellphone-bans.html.
4. Lamb, "Do Phones Belong in Schools?"
5. Christopher Klein, "Guiding Students to Develop a Clear Understanding of Their Cell Phone Use," Edutopia, April 14, 2022, https://www.edutopia.org/article/guiding-students-develop-clear-understanding-their-cell-phone-use/.
6. National Parents Union, "In Case of Emergency: New Survey Finds Why Parents Say Children Should Have Their Cell Phone at School," National Parents Union, September 6, 2024, https://nationalparentsunion.org/2024/09/06/in-case-of-emergency-new-survey-finds-why-parents-parents-say-children-should-have-their-cell-phone-at-school/.

Lesson 9

1. Dana Goldstein, *The Teacher Wars: A History of America's Most Embattled Profession* (Vintage, 2015).
2. Jessica Grose, "People Don't Want to Be Teachers Anymore. Can You Blame Them?" *The New York Times*, September 13, 2023, https://www.nytimes.com/2023/09/13/opinion/teachers-schools-students-parents.html.
3. Mark C. Perna, "No More Teachers: The Epic Crisis Facing Education in 2024," *Forbes*, January 3, 2024, https://www.forbes.com/sites/markcperna/2024/01/03/no-more-teachers-the-epic-crisis-facing-education-in-2024/.
4. Office of Special Education and Rehabilitative Services, *Supporting Child and Student Social, Emotional, Behavioral, and Mental Health Needs*, US Department of Education, 2021, https://www.ed.gov/sites/ed/files/documents/students/supporting-child-student-social-emotional-behavioral-mental-health.pdf.
5. Dana Braga, Kiley Hurst, Shannon Greenwood, Nick Zanetti, and John Carlo Mandapat, "What Public K–12 Teachers Want Americans to Know about Teaching," Pew Research Center, April 4, 2024, https://www.pewresearch.org/social-trends/2024/04/04/what-public-k-12-teachers-want-americans-to-know-about-teaching/.

Lesson 10

1. New York State Department of Health, "COVID-19 Fatalities Tracker," New York State, accessed November 15, 2024, https://coronavirus.health.ny.gov/fatalities-0; USAFacts, "New York Coronavirus Cases and Deaths," USAFacts, accessed November 15, 2024, https://usafacts.org/visualizations/coronavirus-covid-19-spread-map/state/new-york/.

2. Madeline Will, Catherine Gewertz, and Sarah Schwartz, "Did COVID-19 Really Drive Teachers to Quit?" *Education Week*, November 17, 2020, https://www.edweek.org/teaching-learning/did-covid-19-really-drive-teachers-to-quit/2020/11.

3. "Giving Thanks Can Make You Happier," Harvard Health Publishing, August 14, 2021, https://www.health.harvard.edu/healthbeat/giving-thanks-can-make-you-happier.

Lesson 11

1. Emma at Teach Starter, "5 Reasons You Need a Teacher Bestie," TeachS tarter, accessed November 15, 2024, https://www.teachstarter.com/us/blog/5-reasons-you-need-a-teacher-bestie-2/.

Lesson 12

1. Alyson Klein, "1,500 Decisions a Day (At Least!): How Teachers Cope with a Dizzying Array of Questions," *Education Week*, December 6, 2021, https://www.edweek.org/teaching-learning/1-500-decisions-a-day-at-least-how-teachers-cope-with-a-dizzying-array-of-questions/2021/12.

Photo by Eve Prime

About the Author

Anne Richter is currently in her thirty-fifth year of loving her professional life in a classroom. Currently, she teaches life science and STEM in the Tuckahoe Union Free School District in Westchester County, New York. Ms. Richter holds multiple degrees from Columbia University, combining academic expertise and work experience in public health and 7–12 science education, which have afforded her a unique voice while navigating teaching through the unprecedented COVID-19 pandemic and subsequent crises affecting today's teachers and their students. This is Ms. Richter's first nonfiction published work. For more information, please visit www.InOurClassrooms.com.